Medieval Punishments

Skyhorse Publishing books may be purchased in bulk at special discounts for sales promotion, corporate gifts, fund-raising, or educational purposes. Special editions can also be created to specifications. For details, contact the Special Sales Department, Skyhorse Publishing, 307 West 36th Street, 11th Floor, New York, NY 10018 or info@skyhorsepublishing.com.

Visit our website at www.skyhorsepublishing.com.

10 9 8 7 6 5 4 3 2 1

Library of Congress Cataloging-in-Publication Data is available on file.
ISBN: 978-1-62087-618-3

Printed in the United States of America

Medieval Punishments

An Illustrated History of Torture

By William Andrews

Skyhorse Publishing

Preface.

ABOUT twenty-five years ago I commenced investigating the history of obsolete punishments, and the result of my studies first appeared in the newspapers and magazines. In 1881 was issued "Punishments in the Olden Time," and in 1890 was published "Old Time Punishments": both works were well received by the press and the public, quickly passing out of print, and are not now easily obtainable. I contributed in 1894 to the Rev. Canon Erskine Clarke's popular monthly, the *Parish Magazine*, a series of papers entitled "Public Punishments of the Past." The foregoing have been made the foundation of the present volume; in nearly every instance I have re-written the articles, and provided additional chapters. This work is given to the public as my final production on this subject, and I trust it may receive a welcome similar to that accorded to my other books, and throw fresh light on some of the lesser known byways of history.

WILLIAM ANDREWS.

THE HULL PRESS,
August 11th, 1898.

WILLIAM·ANDREWS·&Co
THE·HULL·PRESS

Contents.

Medieval Punishments.

Hanging.

THE usual mode of capital punishment in England for many centuries has been, and still is, hanging. Other means of execution have been exercised, but none have been so general as death at the hands of the hangman. In the Middle Ages every town, abbey, and nearly all the more important manorial lords had the right of hanging, and the gallows was to be seen almost everywhere.

Representatives of the church often possessed rights in respect to the gallows and its victims. William the Conqueror invested the Abbot of Battle Abbey with authority to save the life of any malefactor he might find about to be executed, and whose life he wished to spare. In the days of Edward I. the Abbot of Peterborough set up a gallows at Collingham, Nottinghamshire, and hanged thereon a thief. This proceeding came under the notice of the Bishop of Lincoln, who, with considerable warmth of temper, declared the Abbot had usurped his rights, since he held from the king's predecessors the liberty of the Wapentake of Collingham and the right of executing criminals. The Abbot declared that Henry III. had given him and his successors "Infangthefe and Utfangthefe in all his hundreds and demesnes." After investigation it was decided that the Abbot was in the wrong, and he was directed to take down the gallows he had erected. One, and perhaps the chief reason of the prelate being so particular to retain his privileges was on account of its entitling him to the chattels of the condemned man.

Little regard was paid for human life in the reign of Edward I. In the year 1279, not fewer than two hundred and eighty Jews were hanged for clipping coin, a crime which has brought many to the gallows. The following historic story shows how slight an offence led to death in this monarch's time. In 1285, at the solicitation of Quivil, the Bishop of Exeter, Edward I. visited Exeter to enquire into the circumstances relating to the assassination of Walter Lichdale, a precentor of the cathedral, who had been killed one day when returning from matins. The murderer made his escape during the night and could not be found. The Mayor, Alfred Dunport, who had held the office on eight occasions, and the porter of the Southgate, were both tried and found guilty of a neglect of duty in omitting to fasten the town gate, by which means the murderer escaped from the hands of justice. Both men were condemned to death, and afterwards executed. The unfortunate mayor and porter had not anything to do with the death of the precentor, their only crime being that of not closing the city gate at night, a truly hard fate for neglect of duty.

A hanging reign was that of Henry VIII. It extended over thirty-seven years, and during that period it is recorded by Stow that 72,000 criminals were executed.

In bygone times were observed some curious ordinances for the conduct of the Court of Admiralty of the Humber. Enumerated are the various offences of a maritime character, and their punishment. In view of the character of the court, the punishment was generally to be inflicted at low watermark, so as to be within the proper jurisdiction of the Admiralty, the chief officer of which, the Admiral of the Humber, being from the year 1451, the Mayor of Hull. The court being met, and consisting of "masters, merchants, and mariners, with all others that do enjoy the King's stream with hook, net, or any engine," were addressed as follows : "You masters of the quest, if you, or any of you, discover or disclose anything of the King's secret counsel, or of the counsel of your fellows (for the present you are admitted to be the King's Counsellors), you are to be, and shall be, had down to the low-water mark, where must be made three times, O Yes! for the King, and then and there this punishment, by the law prescribed, shall be executed upon them ; that is, their hands and feet bound, their throats cut, their tongues pulled out, and their bodies thrown into the sea." The ordinances which they were bound to observe, include the following: "You shall inquire, whether any man in port or creek have stolen any ropes, nets, cords, etc., amounting to the value of ninepence; if he have, he must be hanged for the said crimes, at low water-mark." "If any person has removed the anchor of any ships, without licence of the master or mariners, or both, or if anyone cuts the cable of a ship at anchor, or removes or cuts away a buoy; for any of the said offences, he shall be hanged at low water-mark." "All breakers open of chests, or pickers of locks, coffers, or chests, etc., on shipboard, if under the value of one and twenty pence, they shall suffer forty days' imprisonment; but, if above, they must be hanged as aforesaid." "If any loderman takes upon himself the rule of any ship, and she perishes through his carelessness and negligence, if he comes to land alive with two of his company, they two may chop off his head without any further suit with the King or his Admiralty." The sailor element of the population of the olden days was undeniably rude and refractory, the above rules showing that the authorities needed stern and swift measures to repress evildoers of that class.

A curious Derbyshire story is told, taking us back to Tudor times, illustrating the strange superstitions and the power exercised by the nobility in that era. Some three hundred years ago the Peak of Derbyshire was ruled by the iron hand of Sir George Vernon, who, from the boundless magnificence of his hospitality at the famous Hall of Haddon, was known throughout the country round as the "King of the Peak." His "kingly" character was further supported by the stern severity with which he dealt with all cases of dispute or crime that came before him, even when human life was concerned; though it must be added, that if strict, he was also just. The following is an instance of his arbitrary and decisive manner of dealing with the lives of those who came beneath his control, and shows his fondness for the exercise of the summary processes of lynch-law. A wandering pedlar was one morning found dead in an unfrequented part, evidently murdered. He had been hawking his goods about the neighbourhood the previous day, and was in the evening observed to enter a certain cottage, and after that was not again seen alive. No sooner had Sir George Vernon become acquainted with these facts than he caused the body to be conveyed to the hall, where it was laid. The man occupying the cottage where the pedlar had last been seen alive was then summoned to attend at the hall immediately, and on arriving was met by the question, what had become of the pedlar who had gone into his cottage on the previous evening? The fellow repudiated any knowledge of him whatever, when the "King of the Peak" turned round, drew off the sheet which had been placed over the dead body, and ordered that everyone present should successively approach and touch it, declaring at the same time each his innocence of the foul murder. The cottar, who had retained his effrontery until now, shrank from the ordeal, and declined to touch the body, running at once out of the hall, through Bakewell village, in the direction of Ashford. Sir George, coming, as he well might, to the conclusion that the suspicions which had pointed to this man had been well founded, ordered his men to take horse and pursue the murderer, and, overtaking him, to hang him on the spot. They did so; he was caught in a field opposite to where the toll-bar of Ashford stood, and there instantly hanged. The field is still called "Galley Acre," or "Gallows Acre," on this account. It is stated that for this exercise of his powers in summary justice Sir George was called upon to appear at London and answer for the act. When he appeared in court he was the first and second time summoned to surrender as the "King of the Peak," but not replying to these, the third time he was called by his proper title of Sir George Vernon, upon which he acknowledged his presence, stepping forward and crying "Here am I." The indictment having been made out against him under the title of "King of the Peak" it was of no effect, and the worst consequence to Sir George was that he received an admonition. He died in 1567, the possessor of thirty Derbyshire manors, and was buried in Bakewell Church, where his altar tomb remains to this day.

Out of the beaten track of the tourist are the gallows at Melton Ross, Lincolnshire, with their romantic history going back to the time when might and not right ruled the land. According to a legend current among the country folk in the locality long, long ago, some lads were playing at hanging, and trying who could hang the longest. One of the boys had suspended himself from a tree when the attention of his mates was attracted by the appearance on the scene of a three-legged hare (the devil), which came limping past. The lads tried to catch him, and in their eager pursuit forgot the critical position of their companion, and on their return found him dead. The gallows is believed by many to have been erected in remembrance of this event.

The story has no foundation in fact. A hare crossing is regarded not only in Lincolnshire, and other parts of England, but in many countries of the world, as indicating trouble to follow.

In the days of old two notable men held lands in the district, Robert Tyrwhitt of Kettleby and Sir William Ross of Melton, and between them was a deadly feud, the outcome, in 1411, of a

THE GALLOWS AT MELTON ROSS.

slight and obscure question on manorial rights. It was alleged that John Rate, steward of Sir William Ross, had trespassed on lands at Wrawby belonging to Robert Tyrwhitt, digged and taken away turves for firing, felled trees, and cut down brushwood. The dispute was tried by Sir William Gascoigne, but it would appear that this did not altogether meet the requirements of Tyrwhitt. He assembled his men in large numbers and a fight took place with the retainers of Sir William Ross. An action of this kind could not be tolerated even in a lawless age, and the matter was brought before parliament. After long and careful consideration, it was decided that Tyrwhitt was in the wrong, and in the most abject manner he had to beg the pardon of Sir William Ross, but we are told it was merely "lip service."

The hatred of the two families was transmitted from sire to son until the reign of James I., and then it broke out in open warfare. A battle was fought at Melton Ross between the followers of Tyrwhitt and those of the Earl of Rutland, the representative of the Ross family. In the struggle several servants were slain, and the king adopted stringent measures to prevent future bloodshed. He directed, so says tradition, that a gallows be erected at Melton Ross, and kept up for ever, and that if any more deaths should result from the old feud it should be regarded as murder, and those by whom the deadly deed was committed were to be executed on the gallows.

We hear nothing more of the feud after the gallows had been erected, the action of the king being the means of settling a strife which had lasted long and kept the district in turmoil.

The gallows is on the estate of the Earl of Yarborough, and it has been renewed by him, and according to popular belief he is obliged to prevent it falling into decay.

Gallows Customs.

When criminals were carried to Tyburn for execution, it was customary for the mournful procession to stop at the Hospital of St. Giles in the Fields, and there the malefactors were presented with a glass of ale. After the hospital was dissolved the custom was continued at a public-house in the neighbourhood, and seldom did a cart pass on the way to the gallows without the culprits being refreshed with a parting draught. Parton, in his "History of the Parish," published in 1822, makes mention of a public-house bearing the sign of "The Bowl," which stood between the end of St. Giles's High Street, and Hog Lane.

Particulars are given by Pennant and other

writers of a similar custom being maintained at York. It gave rise to the saying, that "The saddler of Bawtry was hanged for leaving his liquor": had he stopped, as was usual with other criminals, to drink his bowl of ale, his reprieve, which was actually on its way, would have arrived in time to save his life.

Robert Dowe, a worthy citizen of London, gave to the vicar and churchwardens of St. Sepulchre's Church, London, fifty pounds, on the understanding that through all futurity they should cause to be tolled the big bell the night before the execution of the condemned criminals in the prison of Newgate. After tolling the bell, the sexton came at midnight, and after ringing a hand-bell, repeated the following lines :—

"All you that in the condemned hold do lie,
Prepare you, for to-morrow you shall die:
Watch all and pray; the hour is drawing near
That you before the Almighty must appear:
Examine well yourselves: in time repent,
That you may not to eternal flames be sent;
And when St. Sepulchre's bell to-morrow tolls,
The Lord above have mercy on your souls!"

Next morning, when the sad procession passed the church on its way to Tyburn, a brief pause was made at the gate of St. Sepulchre's Church, and the clergyman said prayers for the unfortunate criminals, and at the same time the passing-bell tolled its mournful notes.

According to a notice in a recent book by the Rev. A. G. B. Atkinson, Robert Dowe was a merchant tailor, and a benefactor; he assisted John Stow and others. Dowe was born 1522, and died 1612.*

Not a few of the highwaymen who ended their careers at the gallows appear to have been dandies. Swift gives us a picture of one in "Clever Tom Clinch." He says:—

> ". . . While the rabble was bawling,
> Rode stately through Holborn to die of his calling;
> He stopped at the George for a bottle of sack,
> And promised to pay for it—when he came back.
> His waistcoat and stockings and breeches were white,
> His cap had a new cherry ribbon to tie't:
> And the maids at doors and the balconies ran
> And cried 'Lack-a-day! he's a proper young man!'"

On January 21st, 1670, was hanged Claude Duval, a great favourite with the ladies. It is said that ladies of quality, in masks and with tears, witnessed his execution and that he lay in more than royal state at Tangier Tavern, St. Giles's. His epitaph in the centre aisle of St.

* "St Botolph, Aldgate: the Story of a City Parish." 1898.

Paul's, Covent Garden, may be regarded as a model for highwaymen :—

> "Here lies Du Vall : reader, if male thou art,
> Look to thy purse ; if female to thy heart."

Sixteen-string Jack, hanged on November 30th, 1774, was dressed in a "bright pea-green coat, and displayed an immense nosegay."

Frequently rioting occurred at executions, and unpopular criminals would be pelted with missiles, and meet with other indications of disfavour, but usually the sympathies of the populace were with the culprit. Attempts at rescuing criminals would sometimes be made, and soldiers had to be present to ensure order. On the 19th August, 1763, it is stated in "The Annual Register," "A terrible storm made such an impression on the ignorant populace assembled to see a criminal executed on Kennington Common, that the sheriff was obliged to apply to the secretaries of state for a military force to prevent a rescue, and it was near eight o'clock in the evening before he suffered."

Another practice appears to have been to carry the body of an executed criminal to the doors of those who had been the chief cause of the criminal being brought to justice. We read in

"The Annual Register," for 1763. "As soon as the execution of several criminals, condemned at last sessions of the Old Bailey, was over at Tyburn, the body of Cornelius Sanders, executed for stealing about fifty pounds out of the house of Mrs. White, in Lamb Street, Spitalfields, was carried and laid before her door, where great numbers of people assembling, they at last grew so outrageous that a guard of soldiers was sent for to stop their proceedings; notwithstanding which, they forced open the door, pitched out all the salmon-tubs, most of the household furniture, piled them on a heap, and set fire to them, and, to prevent the guards from extinguishing the flames, pelted them off with stones, and would not disperse till the whole was consumed." In the same work for the following year another instance is given. "The criminal," says the record, "condemned for returning from transportation at the sessions, and afterwards executed, addressed himself to the populace at Tyburn, and told them he could wish they would carry his body and lay it at the door of Mr. Parker, a butcher in the Minories, who, it seems, was the principal evidence against him; which, being accordingly done, the mob behaved so riotously before the man's house, that it was no easy matter to disperse them."

Curiosities of the Gallows.

Instances are not wanting of criminals being driven in their own carriages to the place of execution. The story of William Andrew Horne, a Derbyshire squire, as given in the "Nottingham Date Book," is one of the most revolting records of villainy that has come under our notice. His long career of crime closed on his seventy-fourth birthday, in 1759, at the gallows, Nottingham. He had committed more than one murder, but was tried for the death of an illegitimate child of which he was the father. His brother laid the information which at last brought him to justice. This brother requested him to give him a small sum of money so that he might leave the country, but he refused to comply. He then said he should make known his crime, but that did not frighten Horne. He replied, "I'll chance it," and this gave rise to a well-known saying in the Midlands, "I'll chance it as Horne did his neck." He was hanged at Gallows-Hill, Nottingham, and was driven in his carriage by his own coachman. We are told as the gloomy procession ascended the Mansfield Road the white locks of the hoary sinner streamed mournfully in the wind, his head being uncovered and the vehicle open, and the day very tempestuous. He met his doom with a considerable degree of fortitude, in the presence of an immense crowd of spectators, including hundreds of his Derbyshire neighbours and tenantry.*

A year later Earl Ferrers was hanged for the shooting of his own steward. On May 5th, 1760, he was driven from the Tower to Tyburn in a landau drawn by six horses. His lordship was attired in his wedding clothes, which were of a light colour and richly embroidered in silver. He was hanged with a silken rope, and instead of being swung into eternity from a common cart, a scaffold was erected under the gallows, which we think may be regarded as the precursor of the drop. Mr. T. Broadbent Trowsdale contributed to "Bygone Leicestershire" an informing paper on "Laurence Ferrers: the Murderer-Earl."† We reproduce an illustration of the execution from a print of the period.

Some interesting details occur in *Notes and Queries* for May 28th, 1898, respecting "The Colleen Bawn." It is stated that when John

* "The Nottingham Date Book." 1880.

† Andrews's "Bygone Leicestershire." 1892.

Scanlan had been found guilty of the murder of Ellen Hanley, the gentry of the county of Limerick petitioned for a reprieve, which was refused. They next requested that Scanlan be hanged with a silken cord, though whether for its greater dignity or because it offered a possibility of more rapid strangulation in short drop, we cannot tell. The Lord Lieutenant thought hemp would serve the purpose. According to Haydn's "Dictionary of Dates," Scanlan was executed 14th March, 1820.

Mr. Gordon Fraser, of Wigtown, has collected much interesting local lore respecting the town, which was made a royal burgh in 1341. In bygone times it had the distinction of having its own public executioner. According to traditional accounts he held office on somewhat peculiar conditions. The law was, we are told, that this functionary was himself to be a criminal under sentence of death, but whose doom was to be deferred until the advance of age prevented a continuance of his usefulness, and then he was to be hanged forthwith. If, it was said, the town permitted the executioner to die by the ordinary decay of nature, and not by the process of the cord, it would lose for ever the distinguished honour of possessing a public hangman. The story of the last official who held the

EXECUTION OF EARL FERRERS AT TYBURN. *(From a print of the period.)*

tenure of his life upon being able to efficiently despatch his fellows is sufficiently interesting. He was taken ill, and it was seriously contemplated to make sure of having a public hangman in the future by seizing the sick man and hanging him. His friends, hearing of this intention, propped the dying Ketch up in bed, and he, being by trade a shoemaker, had the tools and materials of his trade placed before him. He made a pretence of plying his avocation, and the townsmen, thinking his lease of life was in no danger of a natural termination, allowed him to lie in peace. He then speedily passed away quietly in his bed, and the outwitted burghers found themselves without a hangman, and without hope of a successor.

A good story is told by Mr. Frazer of the last man hanged at Wigtown. His name was Patrick Clanachan, and he was tried and found guilty of horse-stealing. His doom was thus pronounced:—"That he be taken on the 31st August, 1709, between the hours of twelve and two in the afternoon, to the gyppet at Wigtown, and there to hang till he was dead." Clanachan was carried from the prison to the gallows on a hurdle, and, as the people were hurrying on past him to witness his execution, he is said to have remarked, "Tak' yer time, boys, there'll be nae fun till I gang." We have heard a similar anecdote respecting a criminal in London.

At Wicklow, in the year 1738, a man named George Manley was hanged for murder, and just before his execution he delivered an address to the crowd, as follows: "My friends, you assemble to see—what? A man leap into the abyss of death! Look, and you will see me go with as much courage as Curtius, when he leaped into the gulf to save his country from destruction. What will you say of me? You say that no man, without virtue, can be courageous! You see what I am—I'm a little fellow. What is the difference between running into a poor man's debt, and by the power of gold, or any other privilege, prevent him from obtaining his right, and clapping a pistol to a man's breast, and taking from him his purse? Yet the one shall thereby obtain a coach, and honour, and titles; the other, what?—a cart and a rope. Don't imagine from all this that I am hardened. I acknowledge the just judgment of God has overtaken me. My Redeemer knows that murder was far from my heart, and what I did was through rage and passion, being provoked by the deceased. Take warning, my comrades; think what would I now give that I had lived another life. Courageous? You'll say I've killed a man. Marlborough killed his thousands, and Alexander his millions. Marlborough and Alexander, and many others, who have done the like, are famous in history for great men. Aye—that's the case—one solitary man. I'm a little murderer and must be hanged. Marlborough and Alexander plundered countries; they were great men. I ran in debt with the ale-wife. I must be hanged. How many men were lost in Italy, and upon the Rhine, during the last war for settling a king in Poland. Both sides could not be in the right! They are great men; but I killed a solitary man."

It will be seen from the following account, that in the olden time the cost and trouble attending an execution was a serious matter:—

To the Right Honourable the Lord Commissioners of His Majesty's Treasury.

The humble petition of Ralph Griffin, Esq., High Sheriff of the County of Flint, for the present year, 1769, concerning the execution of Edward Edwards, for burglary:—

Sheweth.

That your petitioner was at great difficulty and expense by himself, his clerks, and other messengers and agents he employed in journeys to Liverpool and Shrewsbury, to hire an executioner; the convict being of Wales it was almost impossible to procure any of that country to undertake the execution.

	£	s.	d.
Travelling and other expenses on that occasion -	15	10	0
A man at Salop engaged to do this business. Gave him in part - - - -	5	5	0
Two men for conducting him, and for their search of him on his deserting from them on the road, and charges on inquiring for another executioner - - - - -	4	10	0
After much trouble and expense, John Babington, a convict in the same prison with Edwards, was by means of his wife prevailed on to execute his fellow-prisoner. Gave to the wife - - - - - - -	6	6	0
And to Babington - - - - - -	6	6	0
Paid for erecting a gallows, materials, and labour: a business very difficult to be done in this country - - - - - - -	4	12	0
For the hire of a cart to convey the body, a coffin, and for the burial - - - -	2	10	0
And for other expenses, trouble, and petty expenses, on the occasion at least - -	5	0	0
Total	£49	19	0

Which humbly hope your lordships will please to allow your petitioner, who, etc.

Feasting at funerals in past time was by no means uncommon in Great Britain, and perhaps still lingers in some of the remoter parts of the country. In Scotland until the commencement of the present century before or after executions, civic feasts were often held. After every execution, at Paisley, says the Rev. Charles Rogers, LL.D., the authorities had a municipal dinner. Thomas Potts was hanged at Paisley, 1797, at a cost to the town of £33 5s. 3½d., of which the sum of £13 8s. 10d. was expended on a civic feast, and £1 14s. 3d. on the entertainment of the executioner and his assistants. At Edinburgh, the evening prior to an execution, the magistrates met at Paxton's Tavern, in the Exchange, and made their arrangements over liquor. These gatherings were known as "splicing the rope."*

During the distress which, owing to the scanty harvests of the later years of the last century, prevailed throughout the country, but more especially in the north, attention was drawn to an extremely curious privilege claimed by the public executioner of Dumfries. From old times a considerable portion of the remuneration for his hanging services was in kind, and levied in the following manner. When the farmers and others had set out in the public market their produce of meal, potatoes, and similar provender, the hangman, walking along the row of sacks, thrust into each a large iron ladle, and put the result of each "dip" into his own sack. This tax, from the

* Rogers's "Social Life in Scotland." 1884.

odious occupation of the collector, was regarded by the farmers and factors with particular abhorrence, and numerous attempts were made at different periods to put a stop to the grievous exaction, but the progress of public opinion was so little advanced, and the regard for the ancient trammels of feudal arbitrariness so deep-seated, that not until 1781 was any serious resistance made. In that year a person named Johnston stood upon what he considered his rights, and would allow no acquaintance to be made between his meal and the iron ladle of the Dumfries hangman. The latter, seeing in this the subversion of every fundamental principle of social order, to say nothing of the loss threatened to his means of subsistence, carried his complaint to the magistrates. Consequently the Dumfries Hampden was forthwith haled to prison. He was not, however, long detained there, as his judges were made aware by his threats of action for false imprisonment that they were unaware of the position in which they and the impost stood in the eyes of the law. To remedy this ignorance, and be fore-armed for other cases of resistance, which it was not unlikely to suppose would follow, the Corporation of Dumfries, in the year we have mentioned, had recourse to legal advice. That they obtained was of the highest standing, as they applied to no less a personage than Andrew Crosbie, the eminent advocate, who has been immortalised in the Pleydell of "Guy Mannering." It will be interesting to quote from the document laid before him on this occasion, containing as it does several particulars about the hangman of the town. One part describes the office, duties, and pay of the hangman, "who executes not only the sentences pronounced by the magistrates of the burgh, and of the King's judges on their circuits, but also the sentences of the sheriff, and of the justices of the peace at their quarter sessions. The town has been in use to pay his house rent, and a salary over and above. Roger Wilson, the present executioner, has, since he was admitted, received from the town £6 of salary, and £1 13s. 4d. for a house rent. Over and above this salary and rent, he and his predecessors have been in use of levying and receiving weekly (to wit each market day, being Wednesday,) the full of an iron ladle out of each sack of meal, pease, beans, and potatoes, and the same as to flounders." The history of the impost is next very briefly dealt with, the gist of the information on the subject being that the tax had been levied from a period beyond the memory of the "oldest people" without quarrel or dispute. That the resistance of Johnston was not an isolated instance we likewise learn from this statement of the case, for it says "there appears a fixed resolution and conspiracy to resist and forcibly obstruct the levy of this usual custom," and as the result of the tax according to the executioner's own version amounted to more than £13 annually, it was of sufficient moment to make sound advice desirable. The opinion of Crosbie was that rights obtained by virtue of office, and exercised from time out of mind, were legal, and might very justly be enforced. While commending the imprisonment of the dealer Johnston, he suggested that the process of collection should be made more formal than appears to have been the case in this instance. Officers should assist Jack Ketch in his *rôle* of tax-gatherer, and all preventers should be formally tried by the magistrates. The tax continued to be levied. The farmers either gave up their meal grudgingly, or, refusing, were sent to gaol. In 1796, when the towns-people were in the utmost need of food, riots and tumults arose in Dumfries, and as one means of allaying the popular frenzy it was proposed by the leading member of the Corporation, Provost Haig, that the ladle's harvest should be abolished, and his recommendation was immediately put into effect. The hangman of Dumfries was then one Joseph Tate, who was the last of the officers of the noose connected officially with Dumfries; for the loss of his perquisite he was allowed the sum of £2 yearly. It is satisfactory to learn that the ladle itself, the only substantial relic of this curious custom, is, in all probability preserved at the present time. A foot-note in W. McDowall's valuable "History of Dumfries," says: "The Dumfries hangman's ladle is still to be seen we believe among other 'auld nick-nackets' at Abbotsford." It was for many years lost sight of, till in 1818, Mr. Joseph Train, the zealous antiquary, hunted it out, and, all rusty as it was, sent it as a present to Sir Walter Scott.*

Horrors of the Gallows.

From the following paragraph, drawn from the *Derby Mercury* of April 6th, 1738, we have a striking example of how deplorable was the conduct of the hangman in the olden time. It is by no means a solitary instance of it being mainly caused through drinking too freely:—

* McDowall's "History of Dumfries."

"Hereford, March 25. This day Will Summers and Tipping were executed here for house-breaking. At the tree, the hangman was intoxicated with liquor, and supposing that there were three for execution, was going to put one of the ropes round the parson's neck, as he stood in the cart, and was with much difficulty prevented by the gaoler from so doing."

In bygone times, capital punishment formed an important feature in the every-day life, and was resorted to much more than it now is, for in those "good old times" little regard was paid for human life. People were executed for slight offences. The painful story related by Charles Dickens, in the preface to "Barnaby Rudge," is an example of many which might be mentioned. It appears that the husband of a young woman had been taken from her by the press-gang, and that she, in a time of sore distress, with a babe at her breast, was caught stealing a shilling's worth of lace from a shop in Ludgate Hill, London. The poor woman was tried, found guilty of the offence, and suffered death on the gallows.

We have copied from a memorial in the ancient burial ground of St. Mary's Church, Bury St. Edmunds, the following inscription which tells a sad story of the low value placed on human life at the close of the eighteenth century :—

READER,
Pause at this humble stone it records
The fall of unguarded youth by the allurements of
vice and the treacherous snares of seduction.
SARAH LLOYD.
On the 23rd April, 1800, in the 22nd year of her age,
Suffered a just and ignominious death.
For admitting her abandoned seducer in the
dwelling-house of her mistress, on the 3rd of
October, 1799, and becoming the instrument in
his hands of the crime of robbery and
housebreaking.
These were her last words:
"May my example be a warning to thousands."

Hanging persons was almost a daily occurrence in the earlier years of the present century, for forging notes, passing forged notes, and other crimes which we now almost regard with indifference. George Cruikshank claimed with the aid of his artistic skill to have been the means of putting an end to hanging for minor offences. Cruikshank, in a letter to his friend, Mr. Whitaker, furnishes full details bearing on the subject. "About the year 1817 or 1818," wrote Cruikshank, "there were one-pound Bank of England notes in circulation, and unfortunately there were forged one-pound bank notes in circulation also; and the punishment for passing these forged notes was in some cases transportation for life, and in others DEATH.

"At that time, I resided in Dorset Street, Salisbury Square, Fleet Street, and had occasion to go early one morning to a house near the Bank of England; and in returning home between eight or nine o'clock, down Ludgate Hill, and seeing a number of persons looking up the Old Bailey, I looked that way myself, and saw several human beings hanging on the gibbet, opposite Newgate prison, and, to my horror, two of them were women; and upon enquiring what the women had been hung for, was informed that it was for passing forged one-pound notes. The fact that a poor woman could be put to death for such a minor offence had a great effect upon me, and I at once determined, if possible, to put a stop to this shocking destruction of life for merely obtaining a few shillings by fraud; and well knowing the habits of the low class of society in London, I felt quite sure that in

BANK RESTRICTION NOTE

Specimen of a Bank Note — not to be imitated.

Submitted to the Consideration of the Bank Directors and the inspection of the Public.

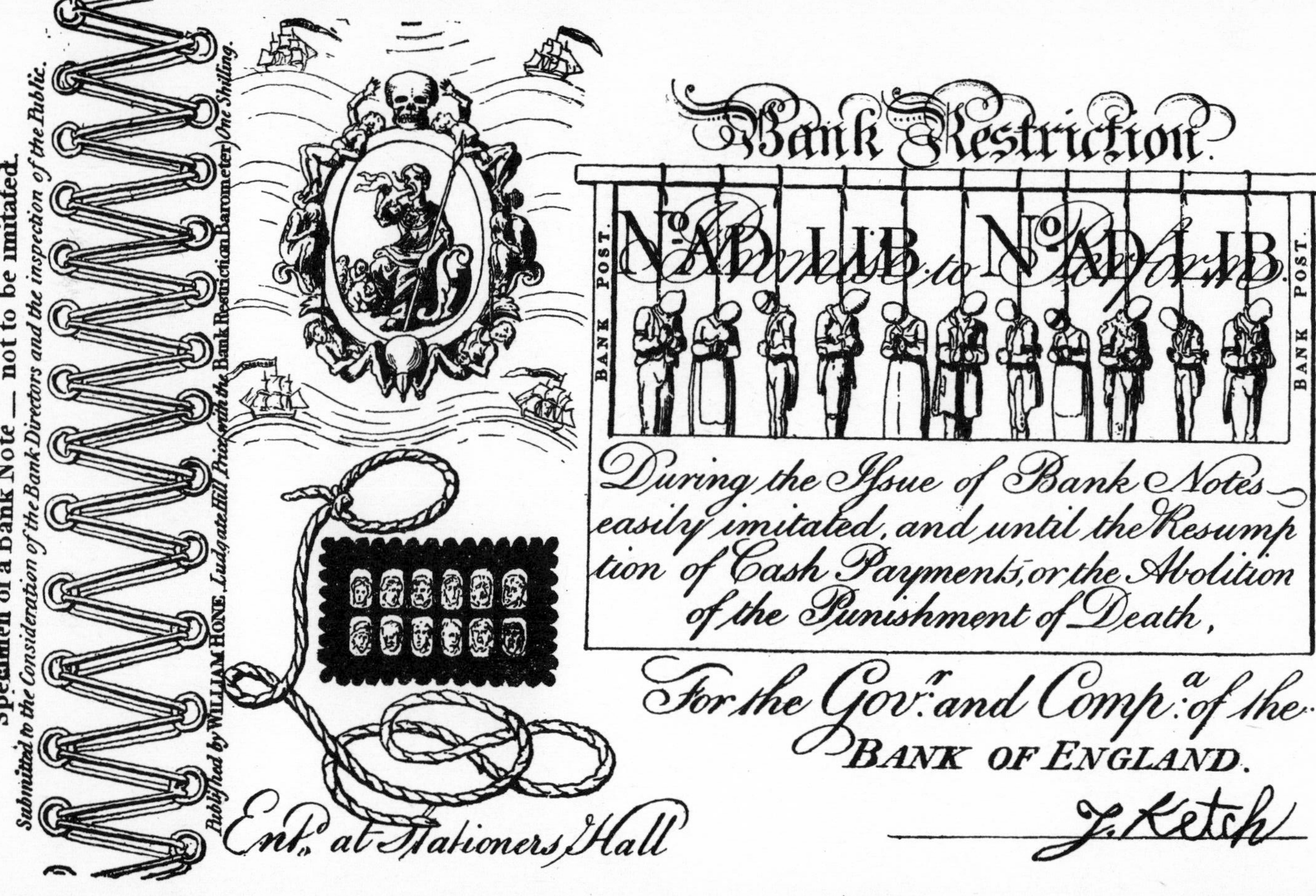

very many cases the rascals who had forged the notes induced these poor ignorant women to go into the gin-shops to get 'something to drink,' and thus *pass* the notes, and hand them the change.

"My residence was a short distance from Ludgate Hill (Dorset Street); and after witnessing the tragic-scene, I went home, and in ten minutes designed and made a sketch of this '*Bank-note not to be imitated*.' About half-an-hour after this was done, William Hone came into my room, and saw the sketch lying on my table; he was much struck with it, and said, 'What are you going to do with this, George?'"

"'To publish it,' I replied. Then he said, 'Will you let me have it?' To his request I consented, made an etching of it, and it was published. Mr. Hone then resided on Ludgate Hill, not many yards from the spot where I had seen the people hanging on the gibbet; and when it appeared in his shop windows, it caused a great sensation, and the people gathered round his house in such numbers that the Lord Mayor had to send the City police (of that day) to disperse the CROWD. The Bank directors held a meeting immediately upon the subject, and AFTER THAT they issued *no more* one-pound notes, and so there was *no more hanging for passing* FORGED *one-pound notes;* not only that, but ultimately no hanging even for forgery. AFTER THIS Sir Robert Peel got a bill passed in Parliament for the 'Resumption of cash payments.' AFTER THIS he revised the Penal Code, and AFTER THAT *there was not any more hanging or punishment of* DEATH *for minor offences.*" We are enabled, by the courtesy of Mr. Walter Hamilton, the author of a favourably-known life of Cruikshank, to reproduce a picture of the "Bank-note not to be imitated." In concluding his letter to Mr. Whitaker, Cruikshank said: "I consider it the most important design and etching that I have ever made in my life; for it has saved the life of thousands of my fellow-creatures; and for having been able to do this Christian act, I am, indeed, most sincerely thankful."

At Nottingham in the olden time the culprits were usually taken to St. Mary's Church, where the officiating clergyman preached their funeral sermon. Next they would inspect their graves, and sometimes even test their capabilities by seeing if they were large enough to hold their remains. Frequently they would put on their shrouds, and in various ways try to show that

THE

BANK RESTRICTION BAROMETER;

OR, SCALE OF EFFECTS ON SOCIETY OF THE

Bank Note System, and Payments in Gold.

BY ABRAHAM FRANKLIN.

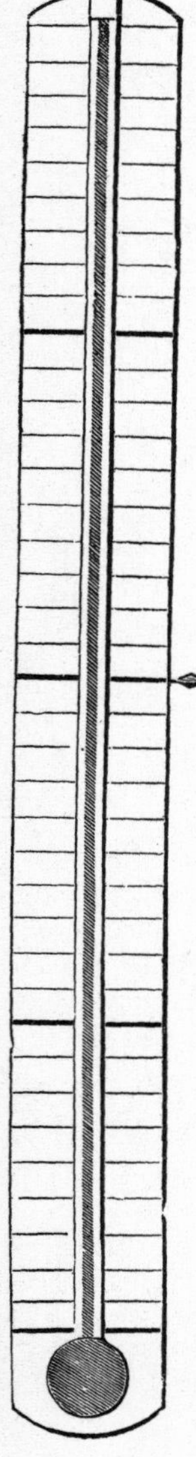

*** *To be read from the words* "BANK RESTRICTION," *in the middle, upwards or downwards.*

NATIONAL PROSPERITY PROMOTED.

10. The Number of useless Public Executions diminished.
9. The Amelioration of the Criminal Code facilitated.
8. The Forgery of Bank Notes at an end.
7. Manufacturers and Journeymen obtain Necessaries and Comforts for their Wages.
6. The Means of Persons with small Incomes enlarged.
5. A Fall of Rents and Prices.
4. The Circulating Medium diminished.
3. Fictitious Capital and False Credit detroyed.
2. Exchanges equalized, and the Gold Coin preserved, if allowed to be freely exported.
1. The Gold Currency restored.

Consequences, if taken off, will be as above:—viz.

THE BANK RESTRICTION.

Consequences of its Operation are as follows:—viz.

1. Disappearance of the legal Gold Coin.
2. The Issues of Bank of England Notes and Country Bank Notes extended.
3. Paper Accommodation, creating False Credit, Fictitious Capital, Mischievous Speculation.
4. The Circulating Medium enormously enlarged.
5. Rents and Prices of Articles of the first Necessity doubled and trebled.
6. The Income and Wages of small Annuitants, and Artizans and Labourers, insufficient to purchase Necessaries for their Support.
7. Industry reduced to Indigence, broken-spirited, and in the Workhouse: or, endeavouring to preserve independence, lingering in despair, committing suicide, or dying broken-hearted.
8. The Temptation to forge Bank of England Notes increased and facilitated.
9. New and sanguinary Laws against Forgery ineffectually enacted,
10. Frequent and useless inflictions of the barbarous Punishment of Death.

GENERAL DISTRESS INCREASED.

they were indifferent to their impending fate. Then they would be conveyed on a cart also containing their coffin to the place of execution some distance from the prison.* Similar usages prevailed in other places.

Public executions always brought together a large gathering of men and women, not always of the lowest order, indeed many wealthy people attended. "The last person publicly executed at Northampton," says Mr. Christopher A. Markham, F.S.A., "was Elizabeth Pinckhard, who was found guilty of murdering her mother-in-law, and who was sentenced to death by Sir John Jervis, on the 27th February, 1852. As a rule all executions had taken place on a Monday, so a rumour was spread that the execution would take place on Monday, the 12th of March; accordingly the people came together in their thousands. They were, however, all disappointed; some of them said they wished they had the under-sheriff and they would let him know what it was to keep honest people in suspense; and one old lady said seriously that she should claim her expenses from the sheriff. However, on Tuesday, the 16th March, Mrs. Pinckhard was executed before an

* Stevenson's "Bygone Nottinghamshire," 1893.

immense number of persons, estimated at ten thousand, the day fixed having by some means or other got known."* The conduct of the crowds which gathered before Newgate and other prisons was long a blot on the boasted civilisation of this country, and there can be little doubt that public executions had a baneful influence on the public.

It will not be without historical interest to state that the last execution for attempted murder was Martin Doyle, hanged at Chester, August 27th, 1861. By the Criminal Law Consolidation Act, passed 1861, death was confined to treason and wilful murder. The Act was passed before Doyle was put on trial, but (unfortunately for him) did not take effect until November 1st, 1861. Michael Barrett, author of the Fenian explosion at Clerkenwell, hanged at Newgate, May 26th, 1868, was the last person publicly executed in England. Thomas Wells (murderer of Mr. Walsh, station-master at Dover), hanged at Maidstone, August 13th, 1868, was the first person to be executed within a prison.

* Markham's "History of Ancient Punishments in Northamptonshire," 1886.

Hanging in Chains.

THE time is not so far distant when the gibbet and gallows were common objects in this country. In old road books, prepared for the guidance of travellers, they are frequently referred to as road marks. Several editions of Ogilby's "Itinirarium Angliæ" were published between 1673 and 1717, and a few passages drawn from this work relating to various parts of England show how frequently these gruesome instruments of death occur:—

"By the Gallows and Three Windmills enter the suburbs of York."

"Leaving the forementioned suburbs [Durham], a small ascent passing between the gallows and Crokehill."

"You pass through Hare Street, etc., and at 13′4 part of Epping Forest, with a gallows to the left."

"You pass Pen-meris Hall, and at 250′4 Hilldraught Mill, both on the left, and ascend a small hill with a gibbet on the right."

"At the end of the city [Wells] you cross a brook, and pass by the gallows."

"You leave Frampton, Wilberton, and Sherbeck, all on the right, and by a gibbet on the left, over a stone bridge."

"Leaving Nottingham you ascend a hill, and pass by a gallows."

Pictures found a prominent place in Ogilby's pages, and we reproduce one of Nottingham.

NOTTINGHAM *(from Ogilby's "Book of Roads.")*

It will be noticed that the gallows is shown a short distance from the town.

It is twenty-six miles from London to East Grinstead, and in that short distance were three of these hideous instruments of death on the highway, in addition to gibbets erected in lonely bylanes and secluded spots where crimes had been committed. "Hangman's Lanes" were by no means uncommon. He was a brave man who ventured alone at night on the highways and byways when the country was beset with highwaymen, and the gruesome gibbets were frequently in sight.

Hanging was the usual mode of capital punishment with the Anglo-Saxons. We give a representation of a gallows *(gala)* of this period taken from the illuminations to Alfric's version of Genesis. It is highly probable that in some instances the bodies would remain *in terrorem* upon the gibbet. Robert of Gloucester, *circa* 1280, referring to his own times, writes:—

"In gibet hii were an honge."

ANGLO-SAXON GALLOWS.

"The habit of gibbeting or hanging in chains the body of the executed criminal near the site of the crime," says Dr. Cox, "with the intention of thereby deterring others from capital offences, was a coarse custom very generally prevalent in mediæval England. Some early assize rolls of the fourteenth century pertaining to Derbyshire that we have consulted give abundant proof of its being a usual habit in the county at that period. In 1341 the bodies of three men were hung in chains just outside Chapel-en-le-Frith, who had been executed for robbery with violence. In the same year a woman and two men were gibbeted on Ashover Moor for murdering one of the King's purveyors." *

An early record of hanging in chains is given in Chauncy's "History of Hertfordshire," It states, "Soon after the King came to Easthampstead, to recreate himself with hunting, where he heard that the bodies hanged here were taken down from the gallowes, and removed a great way from the same; this so incensed the King that he sent a writ, tested the 3rd day of August, Anno 1381, to the bailiffs of this borough, commanding them upon sight thereof, to cause chains to be made, and to hang the bodies in them upon the same gallowes, there to remain so long as one piece might stick to another, according to the judgment; but the townsmen, not daring to disobey the King's command, hanged the dead bodies of their neighbours again to their great shame and reproach, when they could not get any other for any wages to come near the stinking carcases, but they themselves were compelled to do so vile an office." Gower, a contemporary poet, writes as follows :—

* Cox's "Three Centuries of Derbyshire Annals," 1888.

"And so after by the Lawe
He was unto the gibbet drawe,
Where he above all other hongeth,
As to a traitor it belongeth."

Sir Robert Constable was gibbeted above the Beverley-gate, Hull, in 1537, for high treason. "On Fridaye," wrote the Duke of Norfolk, "beying market daye at Hull, suffered and dothe hange above the highest gate of the toune so trymmed in cheynes that I thinke his boones woll hang there this hundrethe yere."

According to Lord Dreghorn, writing in 1774:—"The first instance of hanging in chains is in March, 1637, in the case of Macgregor, for theft, robbery, and slaughter; he was sentenced to be hanged in a chenzie on the gallow-tree till his corpse rot." *

Philip Stanfield, in 1688, was hung in chains between Leith and Edinburgh for the murder of his father, Sir James Stanfield. In books relating to Scotland, Stanfield's sad story has often been told, and it is detailed at some length in Chambers's "Domestic Annals of Scotland."

Hanging in chains was by no means rare from an early period in the annals of England, but

* M'Lauria (Lord Dreghorn) "Arguments and Decisions," etc., Edinburgh, 1774.

according to Blackstone this was no part of the legal judgment. It was not until 1752, by an Act of 25 George II., that gibbeting was legally recognised. After execution by this statute, bodies were to be given to the surgeons to be dissected and anatomized, and not to be buried without this being done. The judge might direct the body to be hung in chains by giving a special order to the sheriff. This Act made matters clear, and was the means of gibbeting rapidly increasing in this country.

A gravestone in the churchyard of Merrington, in the county of Durham, states :—

Here lies the bodies of
John, Jane, and Elizabeth, children of John and Margaret Brass,
Who were murdered the 28th day of January, 1683,
By Andrew Mills, their father's servant,
For which he was executed and hung in chains.
Reader, remember, sleeping
We were slain :
And here we sleep till we must
Rise again.
'Whoso sheddeth man's blood by man shall his blood be shed."
" Thou shalt do no murder."
Restored by subscription in 1789.

The parents of the murdered children were away from home when the awful crime was committed by their farm servant, a young man aged about nineteen, inoffensive, but of somewhat deficient intellect. It is quite clear from the facts which have come down to us that he was insane, for in his confession he stated the devil suggested the deed to his mind, saying, "Kill all, kill all, kill all." The eldest of the family, a daughter, struggled with him for some time, and he was not able to murder her until after her arm was broken. She had placed it as a bolt to a door to secure the safety of the younger members of the family who were sleeping in an inner room. The full particulars of the horrible crime may be found in the pages of Dodd's "History of Spennymoor," published in 1897, and are too painful to give in detail. Some troopers marching from Darlington to Durham seized the culprit, and conveyed him with them. He was tried at Durham, and condemned to be gibbeted near the scene of the murders. Many stories which are related in the district are, we doubt not without foundation in fact. It is asserted that the wretch was gibbeted alive, that he lived for several days, and that his sweetheart kept him alive with milk. Another tale is to the effect that a loaf of bread was placed just within his reach, but fixed on an iron spike that would enter his throat if he attempted to relieve the pangs of hunger with it.

His cries of pain were terrible, and might be heard for miles. The country folk left their homes until after his death. "It is to be hoped," says Mr. Dodd, the local historian, "that the statement about the man being gibbeted alive is a fiction." Some years ago, a local playwright dramatised the story for the Spennymoor theatre, where it drew large audiences.

Long after the body had been removed, a portion of the gibbet remained, and was known as "Andrew Mills's Stob," but it was taken away bit by bit as it was regarded a charm for curing toothache.

Robert and William Bolas were gibbeted on Uckington Heath, near Shrewsbury, in 1723. They had murdered Walter Matthews and William Whitcomb, who had resisted their entering a barn to steal wheat. A popular saying in Shropshire is "Cold and chilly like old Bolas." Its origin is referred back to the time the body of Robert Bolas was hanging in chains. At a public-house not far distant from the place one dark night a bet was made that one of the party assembled dare not proceed alone to the gibbet and ask after the state of Bolas's health. The wager was accepted, and we are told the man undertaking it at once made his way to the spot. Immediately upon this, another of the company, by a short cut, proceeded to the gibbet, and placed himself behind it, and a third, carrying a number of chains, concealed himself in a hedge adjoining the road. Upon arriving at the gibbet, the person undertaking to make the enquiry, screwed up his courage, and timidly said in a low voice, "Well, Bolas, how are you?" Immediately, in a shaky voice, as from a tomb, came the response from the person behind the gibbet, "Cold and chilly, thank you." This unlooked for reply completely upset the valour of the enquirer, and turning tail he fled for the inn with all possible speed. Upon passing the place where the person with the chains was lying, he was followed with a loud rattling and reached his comrades in a most exhausted and frightened condition. Tradition has it that the event terminated in the bold adventurer becoming, and continuing ever afterwards, a lunatic.

When Robert Bolas was awaiting his trial he believed that it would result in an acquittal, and that he would thus be permitted to go home for the corn harvest and get his barley. He was a man of immense strength, and a great source of amusement to his fellow prisoners awaiting trial, before whom, although loaded with heavy chains, he would sing and dance with the most perfect ease. It was upon one of these occasions, when he was in a particularly happy and hopeful mood, that he is reported to have made use of the saying, which is known even to the present day, "I would that these troublesome times were over as I want to go home and get my barley."

A curious story is told to the effect that the corpse of Bolas was taken down from the gibbet by some of his companions and thrown into the river Tern, but that it would not sink. Weights were then tied to it, but still it floated upon the top of the water, and subsequently was again placed upon the gibbet. The part of the river into which it was thrown is still called "Bolas's hole."

In the Town Hall, Rye, Sussex, is preserved the ironwork used in 1742 for gibbeting John Breeds, a butcher, who murdered Allen Grebble, the Mayor of Rye. It appears that Breeds had a dispute about some property with Thomas Lamb, and learning that he was about to see a friend off by a ship sailing to France on the night of March 17th planned his murder. Mr. Lamb, for reasons not stated, changed his mind, and induced his neighbour Mr. Grebble to take his place. On returning home and passing the churchyard, Breeds rushed upon him and mortally wounded him with a knife. The unfortunate man was able to walk home, but shortly expired while seated in his chair. His servant was suspected of murdering him, but Breeds's strange conduct soon brought the crime home to him. He was tried, found guilty, and condemned to death, and to be hung in chains. The gibbet was set up on a marsh situated at the west end of the town, now known as "Gibbet Marsh." Here it stood for many years; but when all the mortal remains had dropped away from the ironwork with the exception of the upper part of the skull, the Corporation took possession of it, and it is now in their custody.

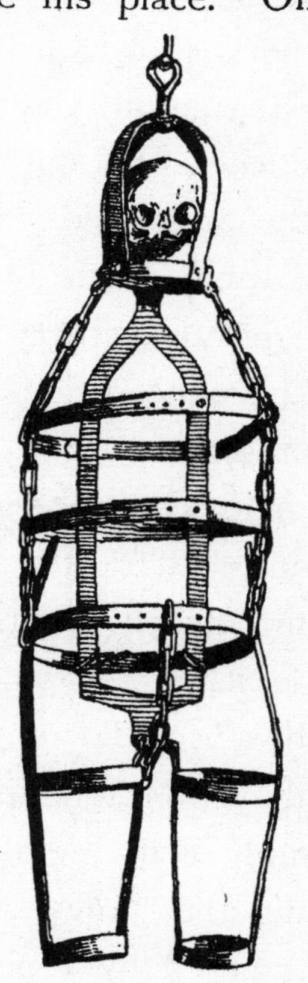

BREEDS'S GIBBET-IRONS, RYE.

Mr. Lewis Evans, has given, in his article on "Witchcraft in Hertfordshire," an account of the murder of John and Ruth Osborn, suspected of witchcraft. Notice had been given at various market towns in the neighbourhood of Tring that on a certain day the man and his wife would be ducked at Long Marston, in Tring Parish. On the appointed day, April 22nd, 1757, says Mr. Evans, Ruth Osborn, and her husband John, sought sanctuary in the church, but the "bigotted and superstitious rioters," who had assembled in crowds from the whole district round, not finding their victims, smashed the workhouse windows and half destroyed it, caught its governor, and threatened to burn both him and the town, and searched the whole premises, even to the "salt box," for the reputed witches in vain. However, they were found at last, dragged from the vestry, and their thumbs and toes having been tied together, they were wrapped in sheets, and dragged by ropes through a pond; the woman was tried first, and as she did not sink, Thomas Colley, a chimney sweep, turned her over and over with a stick. John Osborn, the husband, was then tested in the same way, and the trial was made three times on each of them, with such success, that the woman died on the spot, and the man a few days later. When the experiment was over, Colley went round and collected money from the crowd for his trouble in shewing them such sport.

The coroner's verdict, however, declared that the Osborns had been murdered, and Colley was tried at Hertford Assizes, before Sir William Lee, and having been found guilty of murder, was sent back to the scene of the crime under a large escort of one hundred and eight men, seven officers, and two trumpeters, and was hung on August 24th, 1751, at Gubblecote Cross, where his body swung in chains for many years.*

A Salford woolcomber named John Grinrod (or Grinret), poisoned his wife and two children in September, 1758, and in the following March was hanged and gibbeted for committing the crime. The gibbet stood on Pendleton Moor. It was a popular belief in the neighbourhood :—

> "That the wretch in his chains, each night took the pains,
> To come down from the gibbet—and walk."

As can be easily surmised, such a story frightened many of the simple country folk. It was told to a traveller staying at an hostelry

* Andrews's "Bygone Hertfordshire," 1898.

situated not far distant from where the murderer's remains hung in chains. He laughed to scorn the strange stories which alarmed the country-side, and laid a wager with the publican that he would visit at midnight the gibbet. The traveller said :—

"To the gibbet I'll go, and this I will do,
As sure as I stand in my shoes;
Some address I'll devise, and if Grinny replies,
My wager of course, I shall lose."

We are next told how, in the dark and dismal night, the traveller proceeded without dismay to the gibbet, and stood under it. Says Ainsworth, the Lancashire novelist and poet, from whom we are quoting ;—

"Though dark as could be, yet he thought he could see
The skeleton hanging on high;
The gibbet it creaked; and the rusty chains squeaked;
And a screech-owl flew solemnly by.

The heavy rain pattered, the hollow bones clattered,
The traveller's teeth chattered—with cold—not with fright;
The wind it blew hastily, piercingly, gustily;
Certainly not an agreeable night!

'Ho! Grindrod, old fellow,' thus loudly did bellow,
The traveller mellow—'How are ye, my blade?'—
'I'm cold and I'm dreary; I'm wet and I'm weary;
But soon I'll be near ye!' the skeleton said.

The grisly bones rattled, and with the chains battled,
The gibbet appallingly shook;

On the ground something stirr'd, but no more the man heard,
To his heels, on the instant, he took.
Over moorland he dashed, and through quagmire he plashed,
His pace never daring to slack;
Till the hostel he neared, for greatly he feared
Old Grindrod would leap on his back.
His wager he lost, and a trifle it cost;
But that which annoyed him the most,
Was to find out too late, that certain as fate
The landlord had acted the Ghost."

The tragic story of Eugene Aram has received attention at the hands of the historian, poet, and novelist, and his name is the most notable in the annals of crime in the North of England. In the winter of 1744-5 a shoemaker, named Daniel Clarke, who had recently married, and was possessed of money and other valuables, as it subsequently transpired not obtained in an honourable manner, was suddenly missing, and two of his associates, Richard Houseman and Eugene Aram, were suspected of knowing about his disappearance, and even at their hands foul play was suspected, but it could not be brought home to them. Aram left the town, and in various places followed his calling—that of a school teacher. The mystery of Daniel Clarke remained for some years unsolved, but in 1758 a labourer found at Knaresborough some human bones, and it was suspected that they were Clarke's, and were shown to Houseman, who was supposed to have a knowledge of the missing man, and in an unguarded moment said that they were not those of Clarke. His manner aroused suspicion, and on being pressed he confessed that Clarke was murdered and buried in St. Robert's Cave, and that Aram and himself were responsible for his death. The cave was explored, and the skeleton of the murdered man was found. Aram was arrested at Lynn, where he was an usher in a school, and was esteemed alike by pupils and parents. He stoutly protested his innocence, and undertook his own defence. He read it in court, and it was regarded as a masterpiece of reasoning. It was, however, made clear from the statements of Houseman, who was admitted as king's evidence, that Aram had murdered Clarke for gain when he was in indigent circumstances. The jury returned a verdict of guilty against Aram, and he was condemned to death, and his body to be afterwards hung in chains.

It appears quite clear from a careful consideration of the case that Aram was guilty of the crime.

He attempted, after his trial, to commit suicide

by cutting his arm with a razor in two places, but when discovered, with proper remedies, his failing strength was restored. On the table was found a document giving his reasons for attempting to end his own life. On the morning of his execution he stated that he awoke about three o'clock, and then wrote the following lines :—

Come, pleasing rest, eternal slumber fall,
Seal mine, that once must seal the eyes of all ;
Calm and composed, my soul her journey takes,
No guilt that troubles, and no heart that aches ;
Adieu ! thou sun, all bright like her arise ;
Adieu ! fair friends, and all that's good and wise."

On August 6th, 1759, he was hanged at York, and afterwards his body was conveyed to Knaresborough Forest, where it was gibbeted.

Hornsea people are sometimes called "Hornsea Pennels," after a notorious pirate and smuggler, named Pennel, who murdered his captain and sunk his ship near to the place. He was tried and executed in London for the crimes, and his body, bound round with iron hoops, was sent to Hornsea, in a case marked "glass." The corpse, in 1770, was hung in chains on the north cliff. Long ago the cliff with its gibbet has been washed away by the sea.

On the night of June 8th, 1773, a man named

Corbet, a rat-catcher and chimney-sweep, living at Tring, entered down the chimney the house of Richard Holt, of Bierton, Buckinghamshire, and murdered him in his bed-chamber. For this crime Corbet was hanged and gibbeted in a field not far distant from the house where the murder was committed. The gibbet served as a gallows. A correspondent of the *Bucks Herald* says in 1795 he visited Bierton Feast, and at that period the gibbet was standing, with the skull of the murderer attached to the irons. Some years later the irons were worn away by the action of the swivel from which they were suspended, fell, and were thrown into the ditch, and lost sight of. Francis Neale, of Aylesbury, blacksmith, made the gibbet, or as he calls it in his account the gib, and his bill included entries as follow:—

			£	s.	d.
"July 23, A.D. 1773.	To 6lb. Spikes	- -	0	2	3
" "	Iron for Gib-post	- -	0	16	4
" "	Nails for the Gib	- -	0	4	0
" "	3 hund'd tenter Hooks	-	0	3	0
" "	The Gib	- - -	5	0	0"

These figures were copied from the original accounts by the late Robert Gibbs, the painstaking local chronicler of Aylesbury. This is understood to have been the last gibbet erected in Buckinghamshire.*

Terror and indignation were felt by the inhabitants of the quiet midland town of Derby on Christmas day, in the year 1775, as the news spread through the place that on the previous evening an aged lady had been murdered and her house plundered. An Irishman named Matthew Cocklain disappeared from the town, and he was suspected of committing the foul deed. He was tracked to his native country, arrested, and brought back to Derby. At the following March Assizes, he was tried and found guilty of the crime, sentenced to be hanged, and afterwards gibbeted. His body was for some time suspended in the summer sun and winter cold, an object of fright to the people in the district.

Christmas eve had come round once more, and at a tavern, near the gibbet, a few friends were enjoying a pipe and glass around the cheerful burning yule-log, when the conversation turned to the murderer, and a wager was made that a certain member of the company dare not venture near the grim gibbet at that late hour of night. A man agreed to go, and take with him a basin of

* Sheahan's "History of Buckinghamshire," 1862.

broth and offer it to Matthew Cocklain. He proceeded without delay, carrying on his shoulder a ladder, and in his hand a bowl of hot broth. On arriving at the foot of the gibbet, he mounted the ladder, and put to Cocklain's mouth the basin, saying, "Sup, Matthew," but to his great astonishment, a hollow voice replied, "It's hot." He was taken by surprise; but, equal to the occasion, and at once said, "Blow it, blow it," subsequently throwing the liquid into the face of the suspended body.

He returned to the cosy room of the hostelry to receive the bet he had won. His mate, who had been hid behind the gibbet-post, and had tried to frighten him with his sepulchral speech, admitted that the winner was a man of nerve, and richly entitled to the wager.

It has been asserted by more than one local chronicler that John Whitfield, of Coathill, a notorious north country highwayman, about 1777, was gibbeted alive on Barrock, a hill a few miles from Wetherell, near Carlisle. He kept the countryside in a state of terror, and few would venture out after nightfall for fear of encountering him. He shot a man on horseback in open daylight; a boy saw him commit the crime, and was the means of his identification and conviction. It is the belief in the district that Whitfield was gibbeted alive, and that he hung for several days in agony, and that his cries were heartrending, until a mail-coachman passing that way put him out of his misery by shooting him.

On the night of July 3rd, 1779, John Spencer murdered William Yeadon, keeper of the Scrooby toll-bar, and his mother, Mary Yeadon. The brutal crime was committed with a heavy hedge-stake. The culprit was soon caught, and tried at Nottingham. It transpired that the prisoner was pressed for money, and that the murders were committed to obtain it. He was found guilty, and condemned to be executed at Nottingham, and then his body was to be hung in chains near Scrooby toll-bar. In his hand was placed the hedge-stake with which he had committed the murders. After the body had been suspended a few weeks the body was shot through by the sergeant of a band of soldiers passing that way with a deserter. For the offence he was followed and reported, tried by court-martial, and reduced to the ranks. This disturbance of the body caused its rapid decomposition, and the odour blown over the neighbouring village was most offensive.*

* Stevenson's "Bygone Nottinghamshire," 1893.

Several instances of persons being gibbeted for robbing the mails have come under our notice. In the columns of the *Salisbury Journal* for August 18th, 1783, it is stated :—" The sentence of William Peare for robbing the mail near Chippenham stands unreversed. . . He will be executed at Fisherton gallows, on Tuesday morning, about 11 o'clock, and his body will then be inclosed in a suit of chains, ingeniously made by Mr. Wansborough and conveyed to Chippenham, and affixed to a gibbet erected near the spot where the robbery was committed." The allusion to "unreversed," has reference to the common practice of condemning people to death, and shortly afterwards granting a pardon. The issue of the paper for the following week records that: "On Tuesday morning Peare was executed at Fisherton gallows. . . . The remaining part of the sentence was completed on Wednesday, by hanging the body in Green Lane, near Chippenham, where it now is; a dreadful memento to youth, how they swerve from the paths of rectitude, and transgress the laws of their country." The body of Peare was not permitted to remain long on the gibbet. We see it is stated in a paragraph in the same newspaper under date of November

10th, 1783, that on the 30th of October at night, the corpse was taken away, and it was supposed that this was done by some of his Cricklade friends.

Near the Devil's Punch Bowl, at Hind Head, an upright stone records the murder of a sailor, and the inscription it bears is as under :—

ERECTED
IN DETESTATION OF A BARBAROUS MURDER
committed here on an unknown sailor,
On September 24th, 1786,
BY EDWD. LONEGON, MICHL. CASEY, AND JAS. MARSHALL,
WHO WERE TAKEN THE SAME DAY,
AND HUNG IN CHAINS NEAR THIS PLACE.
"*Whoso sheddeth man's blood, by man shall his blood be shed.*"
—Gen. chap. 9, ver. 6.

And on the back :—

THIS STONE WAS ERECTED BY ORDER AND AT
THE COST OF
JAMES STILWELL, ESQ., OF COSFORD, 1786.
CURSED BE THE MAN WHO INJURETH OR REMOVETH
THIS STONE.

The stone was removed from its original position on the old Portsmouth road, which ran at a higher level, and placed where it now stands some years since.

The three men who committed the crime were arrested at Rake, near Petersfield, and in their possession was found the clothing of the unfortunate sailor. They were tried at Kingston, and found guilty of murder, and condemned to be hanged and gibbeted near where they had committed the foul deed. On April 7th, 1787, the sentence was carried into effect. The gibbet remained for three years, and was then blown down in a gale. The hill is still known as Gibbet Hill.

The murdered man was buried in Thursley churchyard, and over his remains was erected a gravestone, bearing a carving representing three men killing the sailor, and an inscription as follows :—

In Memory of
A generous, but unfortunate Sailor,
Who was barbarously murder'd on Hindhead,
On September 24th, 1786,
By three Villains,
After he had liberally treated them,
And promised them his further Assistance,
On the Road to Portsmouth.

When pitying Eyes to see my Grave shall come,
And with a generous Tear bedew my tomb ;
Here shall they read my melancholy fate—
With Murder and Barbarity complete.
In perfect Health, and in the Flower of Age,
I fell a Victim to three Ruffians' Rage ;

On bended Knees, I mercy strove t'obtain
Their Thirst of Blood made all Entreaties Vain,
No dear Relations, or still dearer Friend,
Weeps my hard lot or miserable End.
Yet o'er my sad remains (my name unknown)
A generous public have inscribed this Stone.

On February 2nd, 1787, two dissolute young men named Abraham Tull and William Hawkins, aged respectively nineteen and seventeen, way-laid and murdered William Billimore, an aged labourer. They stole his silver watch, but were too frightened to continue their search for money which they expected to find, and made a hasty retreat; but they were soon overtaken, and were subsequently, at Reading Assizes, tried and condemned to be gibbeted on Ufton Common within sight of their homes. For many years their ghastly remains were suspended to gibbet posts, much to the terror and annoyance of the people in the district. No attempt was made to remove the bodies, on account of it being regarded as unlawful, until Mrs. Brocas, of Beaurepaire, then residing at Wokefield Park, gave private orders for them to be taken down in the night and buried, which was accordingly done. During her daily drives she passed the gibbeted men and the sight greatly distressed her, and caused her to have them taken down.* The ironwork of the gibbets are in the Reading Museum.

William Lewin, in 1788, robbed the post-boy carrying the letters from Warrington to Northwich, between Stretton and Whitley. He managed to elude the agents of the law for three years, but was eventually captured, tried at Chester, and found guilty of committing the then capital offence of robbing the mail. He was hanged at Chester. Says a contemporary account:—"His body is hung in chains on the most elevated part of Helsby Tor, about eight miles from Chester; from whence it may be conspicuously seen, and, by means of glasses, is visible to the whole county, most parts of Lancashire, Flintshire, Denbighshire, Shropshire, Derbyshire, etc., etc."† About this period there were three gibbets along the road between Warrington and Chester.‡

Only five months after William Lewin had been gibbeted for robbing the mails, almost in the same locality Edward Miles robbed and murdered the post-boy carrying the Liverpool mail-bag to Manchester on September 15th, 1791. For this crime he was hanged, and suspended in chains

* Sharp's "History of Ufton Court," 1892.

† Trial of William Lewin, 1791, Chester, n.d.

‡ Madeley's "Some Obsolete Modes of Punishment," Warrington, 1887.

MILES'S GIBBET IRONS, WARRINGTON MUSEUM.

on the Manchester Road, near "The Twysters," where the murder had been committed. In 1845 the irons in which the body had been encased were dug up near the site of the gibbet, and may now be seen in the Warrington Museum. Our illustration is reproduced from a drawing in Mr. Madeley's work, "Some Obsolete Modes of Punishment." It will be observed the irons which enclosed the head are wanting.

Spence Broughton was tried at York, in 1792, for robbing the mail running between Sheffield and Rotherham. He was found guilty, and condemned to be executed at York, and his body to be hung in chains near the place where the robbery had been committed. The gibbet-post (which was the last put up in Yorkshire), with the irons, the skull, and a few other bones and rags, was standing in 1827-28, when it was taken down.*

We learn from "The Norfolk and Norwich Remembrancer" (1822), that on May 2nd, 1804, the gibbet on which Payne, the pirate, was hung about 23 years previously, upon Yarmouth North Denes, was taken down by order of the Corporation.

Lincolnshire history supplies some curious details

* "Criminal Chronology of York Castle," 1867.

respecting the gibbeting of a man named Tom Otter, in the year 1806. We are told that he was compelled by the old poor law regulations to wed a girl he had injured. He lured her into a secluded spot the day after their marriage, and deliberately murdered her. According to the prevalent custom, Tom Otter's corpse was hung in chains. The day selected for that purpose inaugurated a week of merry-making of the most unseemly character. Booths were pitched near the gibbet, and great numbers of the people came to see the wretch suspended. It is reported that some years later, when the jaw bones had become sufficiently bare to leave a cavity between them, a bird built its nest in this unique position. The discovery of nine young ones therein gave rise to the following triplet still quoted in the neighbourhood:—

> "There were nine tongues within the head,
> The tenth went out to seek some bread,
> To feed the living in the dead."

The gibbet was standing until the year 1850, when it was blown down.

At the Derby March Assizes, 1815, a young man named Anthony Lingard was tried and convicted for murdering Hannah Oliver, a widow, who kept the turnpike-gate at Wardlow Miers, in the parish of Tideswell. The following account of the crime is from the *Derby Mercury*, for March 13th, 1815:—

"On Saturday morning, Anthony Lingard, the younger, aged 21, was put to the bar, charged with the murder (by strangulation) of Hannah Oliver, a widow woman, aged 48 years, who kept the turnpike gate at Wardlow Miers, in the parish of Tideswell, in this county.

It appeared in evidence that the prisoner committed the robbery and murder in the night of Sunday the 15th of January last; that he took from the house several pounds in cash and notes, and a pair of new woman's shoes; that immediately after the deed was perpetrated, he went to a young woman in the neighbourhood, who was pregnant by him, and offered to give her some money with a view to induce her to father the child upon some other person; that he gave her the shoes, and also some money; but it being rumoured that Hannah Oliver had been murdered, and that a pair of shoes had been taken from her, the young woman returned the shoes to the prisoner, who said she had no occasion to be afraid, for that he had had them of a person in exchange for a pair of stockings. The shoes, however, were returned to him; and the evidence adduced in respect to them, as well as in respect to a great variety of circumstances connected with the horrid transaction, was given in such a very minute detail of corroborative and satisfactory proofs, as to leave no doubt in the minds of everyone that the prisoner was the person who had committed the murder, independent of his own confession, which was taken before the magistrates, previous to his committal.

The trial on the part of the prosecution being closed, and

the prisoner not having any witness to call, the learned judge carefully summed up the evidence to the jury, who after a few minutes returned a verdict of guilty.

His Lordship then passed the awful sentence of the law upon the prisoner, which was done by the learned judge in the most solemn and impressive manner, entreating him to make the best use of his time, and to prepare himself during the short period he had to live, for the great change he was about to undergo.

Since his condemnation he conducted himself with greater sobriety than he had manifested before his trial; but his temper was obstinate, and his mind lamentably ignorant: and being totally unacquainted with religious considerations, he exhibited very imperfect signs of real penitence, and but little anxiety respecting his future state. He acknowledged the crime for which he was about to suffer the sentence of the law, but was reluctantly induced to pronounce his forgiveness of the young woman who was the principal evidence against him.

At 12 o'clock yesterday he was brought upon the drop in front of the County gaol, and after a short time occupied in prayer with the chaplain (who had previously attended him with the most unremitting and tender assiduity), he was launched into eternity. He met his fate with a firmness which would deserve the praise of fortitude if it was not the result of insensibility. He appeared but little agitated or dejected by his dreadful situation.

Let the hope be encouraged that his example may operate as a warning to those among the multitude of spectators, who might not before feel all the horror with which vice ought to be regarded. When wickedness is thus seen not in its allurements, but in its consequences, its true nature is evidenced. It is always the offspring of ignorance and folly, and the parent of long enduring misery.

Before the Judge left the town, he directed that the body of Lingard should be hung in chains in the most convenient place near the spot where the murder was committed, instead of being dissected and anatomized."

The treasurer's accounts for Derbyshire, for 1815-16, show, says Dr. Cox, that the punishment of gibbeting involved a serious inroad on the county finances. The expenses for apprehending Anthony Lingard amounted to £31 5s. 5d., but the expenses incurred in the gibbeting reached a total of £85 4s. 1d., and this in addition to ten guineas charged by the gaoler for conveying the body from Derby to Wardlow.*

A paragraph in Rhodes's "Peak Scenery," first published in 1818, is worth reproducing:—"As we passed along the road to Tideswell," writes the author, "the villages of Wardlow and Litton lay on our left. . . . Here, at a little distance on the left of the road, we observed a man suspended on a gibbet, which was but newly erected. The vanity of the absurd idea of our forefathers, in thinking that a repulsive object of this kind would act as a deterrent of crime, was strikingly shown in the case of this Wardlow gibbet." It is related of Hannah Pecking, of Litton, who was hung on

* Cox's "Three Centuries of Derbyshire Annals," 1888.

March 22nd, 1819, at the early age of sixteen, for poisoning Jane Grant, a young woman of the same village, that she "gave the poison in a sweet cake to her companion, as they were going to fetch some cattle out of a field, near to which stood the gibbet-post of Anthony Lingard."

The gibbet was taken down on April 10th, 1826, by order of the magistrates, and the remains of Lingard buried on the spot. We give a drawing of Lingard's gibbet-cap, which is now in the museum at Belle Vue, Manchester.

The Rev. Dr. Cox contributed to the columns of *The Antiquary*, for November, 1890, some important notes on this theme. "It was usual," says Dr. Cox, "to saturate the body with tar before it was hung in chains, in order that it might last the longer. This was done with the bodies of three highwaymen about the middle of last century, gibbeted on the top of the Chevin, near Belper, in Derbyshire. They had robbed the North Coach when it was changing horses at the inn at Hazelwood, just below the summit of the Chevin. After the bodies had been hanging there for a few weeks, one of the friends of the criminals set fire at night time to the big gibbet that bore all three. The father of our aged informant, and two or three others of the cottagers near by, seeing a glare of light, went up the hill, and there they saw the sickening spectacle of the three bodies blazing away in the darkness. So thoroughly did the tar aid this cremation that the next morning only the links of the iron remained on the site of the gibbet."

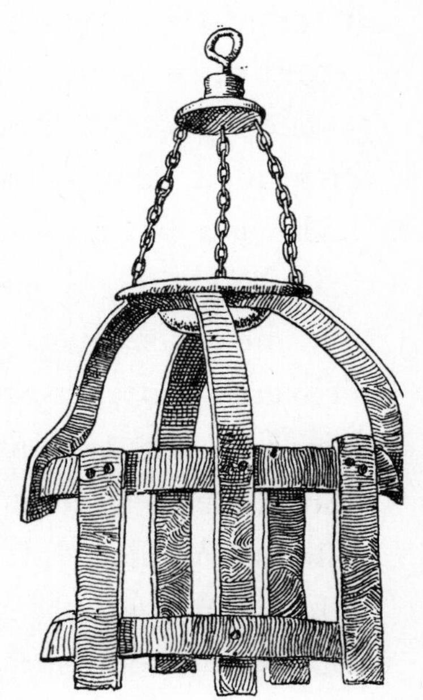

LINGARD'S GIBBET-CAP.

On the high road near Brigg, in 1827, a murder was committed by a chimney-sweep. At the Lincoln Assizes he was condemned to be hanged, and hung in chains on the spot where the tragedy occurred. The inhabitants of Brigg petitioned against the gibbeting, as it was so near the town, and consequently that part of the sentence was remitted.

A strike occurred at Jarrow Colliery, in 1832, and Mr. Nicholas Fairles, one of the owners, was a magistrate for the county of Durham, the only one in the district, and he took an active part in preserving peace during the troublesome time.

He was seventy-one years of age, and greatly esteemed for his kindly disposition and high moral character. On June 11th he had been transacting some business at the Colliery, and was riding home to South Shields on his pony. When he had reached a lonely place, two men attacked him, dragging him from his horse, because he refused to give them money. They then felled him to the ground with a bludgeon, and as he lay helpless on the ground, heavy stones were used to end his life.

He was left for dead, but on being found and carried to a neighbouring house, it was discovered that he was alive, and after a few hours he recovered consciousness, and was able to give the names of the two men who had attempted to murder him, whom he knew, and who were Jarrow colliers, William Jobling and Ralph Armstrong. After lingering a few days, Mr. Fairles died. Jobling was soon caught, but Armstrong escaped, and was never brought to justice. Jobling was tried at Durham Assizes, and condemned to be hanged and gibbeted. On August 3rd he was executed at Durham, and his body was subsequently escorted by fifty soldiers and others to Jarrow Slake, and set up on a gibbet 21 feet high. The post was fixed into a stone, weighing about thirty hundred-weight, and sunk into the water a hundred yards from the high-water mark, and opposite the scene of the tragedy. The gruesome spectacle was not permitted to remain, for on the night of the 31st of the same month it was erected it was taken down, it is supposed, by some of his fellow workmen, and the body was quietly buried in the south-west corner of Jarrow churchyard. It only remains to be added that during the construction of the Tyne Dock, the iron framework in which Jobling's body was suspended was found, and was in 1888 presented by the directors of the North Eastern Railway Company to the Newcastle Society of Antiquaries. On 14th April, 1891, passed away at the advanced age of 96, Jobling's widow, and it has been stated, with her death the last personal link with the gibbet was severed.

The last man gibbeted in this country was James Cook, a bookbinder, at Leicester. He was executed for the murder of John Paas, a London tradesman, with whom he did business. Cook's body was suspended on a gibbet thirty-three feet high, on Saturday, August 11th, 1832, in Saffron Lane, Aylestone, near Leicester. The body was soon taken down, and buried on the spot where the gibbet stood, by order of the Secretary of State, to put a stop to the disturbances caused by the crowds of people visiting the place on a Sunday.*

Some little time before the execution of a criminal who was also condemned to be hung in chains, it was customary for the blacksmith to visit the prison and measure the victim for the ironwork in which he was to be suspended.

Hanging Alive in Chains.

Nearly every district in England has its thrilling tale of a man hanging alive in chains. Some writers affirm the truth of the story, while others regard it as merely fiction. We are not in a position to settle the disputed question. Blackstone, in his "Commentaries," published in 1769, clearly states that a criminal was suspended in chains after execution. Holinshed, who died about the year 1580, in his famous "Chronicle of England," a work which supplied Shakespeare with materials for historical dramas, states :—"In wilful murder done upon pretended (premeditated) malice, or in anie notable robbery, the criminal is either hanged alive in chains near the place where the act was committed, or else, upon com-

* See "Bygone Leicestershire," edited by William Andrews, 1892.

passion taken, first strangled with a rope, and so continueth till his bones come to nothing. Where wilful manslaughter is perpetrated, besides hanging, the offender hath his right hand commonly stricken off."

We glean an important item from "England's Mourning Garment," written by Henry Chettle, a poet and dramatist, born about the year 1540, and who died in 1604. He lived in the days of Queen Elizabeth. "But for herselfe," wrote Chettle, "she was alwayes so inclined to equitie that if she left Justice in any part, it was in shewing pittie; as in one generall punishment of murder it appeared; where-as before time there was extraordinary torture, as hanging wilfull murderers alive in chains; she having compassion like a true Shepheardesse of their soules, though they were often erring and utterly infected flock, said their death satisfied for death; and life for life was all that could be demanded; and affirming more, that much torture distracted a dying man." This subject is fully discussed in *Notes and Queries*, 4th series, volumes X. and XI. A work entitled "Hanging in Chains," by Albert Hartshorne, F.S.A., (London, 1891), contains much out-of-the-way information on this theme.

Bewick, the famous artist and naturalist, in his pictures of English scenery introduced the gibbet "as one of the characteristics of the picturesque."

The old custom of hanging the bodies of criminals in chains was abolished by statute on July 25th, 1834, and thus ends a strange chapter in the history of Old England.

THE GIBBET (*from Bewick's "British Birds."*)

Hanging, Drawing, and Quartering.

HANGING, drawing, and quartering, with their attendant horrors, have been termed "godly butchery," on account of the divine authority which was adduced to support their continuance. Lord Coke finds in the Bible a countenance for each of the horrid details of the punishment. We see that the texts supposed to bear upon the subject are raked from all parts of the Scriptures with great ingenuity, but with, in our modern eyes, not much of either humanity or probability of there being anything more than a forced reference. The sentence on traitors was pronounced as follows: "That the traitor is to be taken from the prison and laid upon a sledge or hurdle [in earlier days he was to be dragged along the surface of the ground, tied to the tail of a horse], and drawn to the gallows or place of execution, and then hanged by the neck until he be half dead, and then cut down; and his entrails to be cut out of his body and burnt by the executioner; then his head is to be cut off, his body to be divided into quarters, and afterwards his head and quarters to be set up in some open places directed." The headsman, or hangman, commonly sliced open the chest and cut thence the heart, plucking it forth and holding it up to the populace, saying, "Behold the heart of a traitor." The members were disposed on the gates of the cities, and in London on London Bridge, or upon Westminster Hall.

It is asserted that this mode of capital punishment was first inflicted in 1241, on William Marise, pirate, and the son of a nobleman.

For a long period this disgusting punishment was the penalty for high treason. A late instance, and the last in the provinces, occurred at Derby in 1817. At this period distress prevailed to an alarming extent in many parts of the country, but no where was it more keenly felt than in the Midland counties. At the instigation of paid government spies, the poor, suffering people were urged to overthrow the Parliament. The plot was planned in a public house called the White Horse, at Pentrich, Derbyshire. A few half-starved labouring men took part in the rising, being assured by the perjured spies that it would simultaneously occur throughout the breadth and length of the land, and that success must crown their efforts. The deluded men had not advanced far before they were scattered by the Yeomanry, and the chief movers taken prisoners. It was the object of the government to terrify the public and cripple all attempts at obtaining reform. Four judges were sent to Derby to try the poor peasants for rebellion, and commenced their duties on the 15th and ended them on October 25th. Three of the ringleaders, Jeremiah Brandreth, William Turner, and Isaac Ludlam, were found guilty of high treason, and the capital sentence passed upon them ; the greater part of the other prisoners were condemned to transportation. Little time was lost in carrying out the sentence ; the death warrant for the execution was signed on November 1st by the Prince Regent, and it remitted only quartering, and directed that the three men be hung, drawn, and beheaded. It appears that the High Sheriff, after consultation with the surgeon of the prison and other officials, proposed taking off the heads of the unfortunate men with a knife, and the operation to be performed by a person skilled in anatomy. On this being brought under the notice of the authorities in London, it was, however, decided that the execution should be carried out according to old usage with the axe. Bamford, a blacksmith, of Derby, was entrusted with an order for two axes, to be made similar to the one used at the Tower. They measured eight and a half inches across the edge and were one foot long. On the morning of November 7th, before execution, the three men received Sacrament. The town blacksmith knocked off the irons by which they were loaded, and substituted others that were fitted with locks, so that they might easily be removed. A simply made hurdle was then brought in the prison-yard, and on it they were pulled by a horse to the gallows. It was so roughly constructed that the poor fellows had to be held to keep them on it. On mounting the scaffold in front of the gaol," says Dr. Cox, to whom we are indebted for many details in this chapter, "Brandreth exclaimed, 'It is all Oliver and Castlereagh ;' Turner, following him, also called out, 'This is all Oliver and the Government ; the Lord have mercy on my soul.' They hung from the gallows for half-an-hour. On the platform, in front of the gallows, was placed the block and two sacks of sawdust, and on a bench two axes, two sharp knives, and a basket. The block was a long piece of timber supported at each end by pieces a foot high, and having a small batten nailed across the upper end for the neck to rest upon. The body of Brandreth was first taken down from the gallows, and placed face downwards on the block. The executioner, a muscular Derbyshire coal miner, selected by the sheriff for his proficiency in wielding the pick, was masked, and his name kept a profound secret. Brandreth's neck received only one stroke, but it was not clean done, and the assistant (also masked) finished it off with a knife. Then the executioner laid hold of the head by the hair, and holding it at arm's length, to the left, to the right, and in front of the scaffold, called out three times—'Behold the head of the traitor, Jeremiah Brandreth.' The other two were served in like manner. Turner's neck received one blow and the knife had to be applied, but Ludlam's head fell at once. The scaffold was surrounded by a great force of cavalry with drawn swords, and several companies of infantry were also present. The space in front of the gaol was densely packed with spectators." * "When the first stroke of the axe was heard," says an eyewitness, "there was a burst of horror from the

* Cox's "Three Centuries of Derbyshire Annals." 1888.

crowd, and the instant the head was exhibited there was a terrifying shriek set up, and the multitude ran violently in all directions, as if under the influence of a sudden frenzy." *

The poet Shelley is said to have witnessed the painful spectacle. On the previous day had passed away in childbirth the Princess Charlotte. The two circumstances formed the subject of an able pamphlet, drawing a contrast between the deaths, and furnishing a description of the scene within and without the prison at Derby. "When Edward Turner (one of those transported)," says Shelley, "saw his brother dragged along upon the hurdle, he shrieked horribly, and fell in a fit, and was carried away like a corpse by two men. How fearful must have been their agony sitting in solitude that day when the tempestuous voice of horror from the crowd told them that the head so dear to them was severed from the body! Yes, they listened to the maddening shriek which burst from the multitude; they heard the rush of ten thousand terror-stricken feet, the groans and hootings which told them that the mangled and distorted head was then lifted in the air." The title of Shelley's pamphlet is "We pity the

* *The Examiner.*

Plumage, but forget the Dying Bird. An Address to the People on the Death of the Princess Charlotte. By the Hermit of Marlow."

On same night the three executed men were buried without any religious service in one grave in the churchyard of St. Werburgh, Derby.

When Dr. Cox was preparing for the press his "Three Centuries of Derbyshire Annals," he saw the block on which these men were beheaded and supplies a description of it as follows: "It consists of two two and a half inch planks fastened together; it is six feet six inches long by two feet wide. Six inches from one end a piece of wood is nailed across three inches high. The whole is tarred over, but the old warder drew our attention to the fact that, though the cell where it is kept is very dry, the wood is still in places damp. It is a gaol tradition that the blood of these unhappy men shed in 1817 has never and will never dry."

On May 1st, 1820, the Cato Street Conspirators were, after death by hanging, beheaded. This is the latest instance of the ancient custom being maintained in this country. In connection with this subject we may perhaps be permitted to draw attention to a chapter by us in "England in the Days of Old" (1897), entitled "Rebel

Heads on City Gates;" it includes much curious information bearing on this theme.

We must not omit to state that the great agitator against the continuance of the barbarities of hanging, drawing and quartering was Sir Samuel Romilly, who in the reign of George III., brought upon himself the odium of the law-officers of the Crown, who declared he was "breaking down the bulwarks of the constitution." By his earnest exertions, however, the punishment was carried out in a manner more amenable to the dictates of mercy and humanity.

Pressing to Death.

ONE of the most barbarous and cruel of the punishments of our English statutes was that distinguished by the name of *Peine forte et dure*, or pressing to death with every aggravation of torture. It was adopted as a manner of punishment suitable to cases where the accused refused to plead, and was commuted about the year 1406 from the older method of merely starving the prisoner to death. At that time the alteration was considered to be decidedly according to the dictates of humanity and mercy, as the sooner relieving the accused from his sufferings. Such was the small value set upon human life in those dark days of British justice.

The manner in which this exceedingly great torture was inflicted was as follows: "That the prisoner shall be remanded to the place from whence he came, and put in some low, dark room, and there laid on his back, without any manner of covering except a cloth round his middle; and that as many weights shall be laid upon him as he can bear, *and more;* and that he shall have no more sustenance but of the worst bread and water, and that he shall not eat the same day on which he drinks, nor drink the same day on which he eats; and he shall so continue till he die." At a later period, the form of sentence was altered to the following: "That the prisoner shall be remanded to the place from whence he came, and put in some low, dark room; that he shall lie without any litter or anything under him, and that one arm shall be drawn to one quarter of the room with a cord, and the other to another, and that his feet shall be used in the same manner, and that as many weights shall be laid on him as he can bear, and more. That he shall have three morsels of barley bread a day, and that he shall have the water next the prison, so that it be not current, and that he shall not eat," etc. The object of this protracted punishment was to allow the victim, at almost every stage of the torture, to plead, and thus allow the law to take its ordinary course. The object of the persons who have refused to plead was, that any person who died under the *Peine forte et dure* could transmit his estates to his children, or will them as he desired; whereas, if he were found guilty, they would be forfeited to the Crown. In connection with this, it may be mentioned that when the practice of pressing to death had become nearly extinct, prisoners who declined to plead were tortured, in order to compel them to do so, by twisting and screwing their thumbs with whipcord.

In 1721, a woman named Mary Andrews was subjected to this punishment. After bearing with fortitude the first three whipcords, which broke from the violence of the twisting, she submitted to plead at the fourth.

Baron Carter, at the Cambridge Assizes, in 1741, ordered a prisoner, who refused to plead, to have his thumbs twisted with cords, and when that was without avail, inflicted the higher penalty of pressing. Baron Thompson, about the same time, at the Sussex Assizes, treated a prisoner in a precisely similar manner.

A like method was pursued in 1721, with Nathaniel Hawes, a prisoner who refused to plead; when the cord proved inefficacious, a weight of 250 pounds was laid upon him, after which he decided to plead. The same year seems prolific of cases of this character, there being particulars of an instance in the *Nottingham Mercury* of January 19th, 1721. They are included in the London news, and are as follow:

"Yesterday the sessions began at the Old Bailey, where several persons were brought to the bar for highway robbery, etc. Among them were the highwaymen lately taken at Westminster, two of whom, namely, Thomas Green, *alias* Phillips, and Thomas Spiggot, refusing to plead, the court proceeded to pass the following sentence upon them: 'that the prisoner shall be,' etc. [the usual form, as given above]. The former, on sight of the terrible machine, desired to be carried back to the sessions house, where he pleaded not guilty. But the other, who behaved himself very insolently to the ordinary who was ordered to attend him, seemingly resolved to undergo the torture. Accordingly, when they brought cords, as usual, to tie him, he broke them three several times like a twine-thread, and told them if they brought cables he would serve them after the same manner. But, however, they found means to tie him to the ground, having his limbs extended; but after, enduring the punishment for an hour, and having three or four hundredweight put on him, he at last submitted to plead, and was carried back, when he pleaded not guilty."

The Rev. Mr. Willette, the ordinary of the

prison, in 1776, published the "Annals of Newgate," and from these we learn further particulars of the torture of the highwayman, Thomas Spiggot. "The chaplain found him lying in the vault upon the bare ground, with 350 pounds weight upon his breast, and then prayed with him, and at several times asked him why he should hazard his soul by such obstinate kind of self-murder. But all the answer that he made was, 'Pray for me; pray for me.' He sometimes lay silent under the pressure as if insensible to the pain, and then again would fetch his breath very quick and short. Several times he complained that they had laid a cruel weight upon his face, though it was covered with nothing but a thin cloth, which was afterwards removed and laid more light and hollow; yet he still complained of the prodigious weight upon his face, which might be caused by the blood being forced up thither and pressing the veins so violently as if the force had been externally on his face. When he had remained for half-an-hour under this load, and fifty pounds weight more laid on, being in all four hundred, he told those who attended him he would plead. The weights were at once taken off, the cords cut asunder; he was raised up by two men, some brandy put into his mouth to revive him, and he was carried to take his trial." The practice of *Peine forte et dure* gave the name of "Press-yard" to a part of Newgate, and the terrible machine above referred to was probably in the form of a rack.

We require to go further back to find instances of a fatal termination to the punishment. Such a case occurred in 1676. One Major Strangeways and his sister held in joint possession a farm, but the lady becoming intimate with a lawyer named Fussell, to whom the Major took a strong dislike, he threatened that if she married the lawyer he would, in his office or elsewhere, be the death of him. Surely, Fussell was one day found shot dead in his London apartments, and suspicion at once fell upon the officer, and he was arrested. At first he was willing to be subjected to the ordeal of touch, but when placed upon trial, resolved not to allow any chance of his being found guilty, and so refused to plead, in order that his estates might go to whom he willed. Glynn was the Lord Chief Justice on this occasion, and in passing the usual sentence for *Peine forte et dure*, used instead of the word "weights," as above, the words "as much iron and stone as he can bear," doubtless to suit the prison convenience, and make the sentence perfectly legal. He was to have three morsels of barley bread every alternate day, and three draughts of "the water in the next channel to the prison door, but of no spring or fountain water," the sentence concluding, "and this shall be his punishment till he die." This was probably on the Saturday, for on the Monday morning following, it is stated, the condemned was draped in white garments, and also wore a mourning cloak, as though in mourning for his own forthcoming death. It is curious to notice that his friends were present at his death, which was so much modified from the lengthy process that his sentence conveys as to be in fact an execution, in which these same friends assisted. They stood "at the corner of the press," and when he gave them to understand that he was ready, they forthwith proceeded to pile stone and iron upon him. The amount of weight was insufficient to kill him, for although he gasped, "Lord Jesus, receive my soul," he still continued alive until his friends, to hasten his departure, stood upon the weights, a course which in about ten minutes placed him beyond the reach of the human barbarity which imposed upon friendship so horrible a task.

In 1827, an Act was passed which directs the court to enter a plea of "not guilty," when a prisoner refuses to plead. It is surprising that the inhuman practice of pressing to death should have lingered so long. In this chapter we have only given particulars of a few of the many cases which have come under our notice in the legal byways of old England.

Drowning.

AMONG the nations of antiquity, drowning was a very common mode of execution. Four-and-a-half centuries before the birth of Christ, the Britons inflicted death by drowning in a quagmire. In Anglo-Saxon times women found guilty of theft were drowned. For a long period in the Middle Ages, the barons and others who had the power of administering laws in their respective districts possessed a drowning pit and a gallows.

Drowning was a punishment of King Richard of the Lion Heart, who ordained by a decree that it should be the doom of any soldier of his army who killed a fellow-crusader during the passage to the Holy Land.

The owner of Baynard's Castle, London, in the reign of John, had the power of trying criminals, and his descendants long afterwards claimed the privilege, the most valued of which was the right of drowning, in the Thames, traitors taken within the limits of his territory.*

* Pike's "History of Crime in England," 1873.

Bearing on this subject the annals of Sandwich supply some important information. It is recorded, that in the year 1313, "a presentment was made before the itinerant Justices at Canterbury, that the prior of Christ Church had, for nine years, obstructed the high road leading from Dover Castle to Sandwich by the sea-shore by a water-mill, and the diversion of a stream called the Gestlyng, where felons condemned to death within the hundred should be drowned, but could not be executed that way for want of water. Further, that he raised a certain gutter four feet, and the water that passed that way to the gutter ran to the place where the convicts were drowned, and from whence their bodies were floated to the river, and that after the gutter was raised the drowned bodies could not be carried into the river by the stream, as they used to be, for want of water." *

Drowning was not infrequently awarded as a matter of leniency, and as a commutation of what were considered more severe forms of death. We have an instance of such a case in Scotland in 1556, when a man who had been found guilty of theft and sacrilege was ordered to be put to death

* Boys's "History of Sandwich."

by drowning "by the Queen's special grace." At Edinburgh, in 1611, a man was drowned for stealing a lamb; and in 1623 eleven gipsey women were condemned to be drowned at Edinburgh in the Nor' Loch. On the 11th May, 1685, Margaret M'Lachlan, aged sixty-three years, and Margaret Wilson, a girl of eighteen years, were drowned in the waters of Blednoch, for denying that James VII. of Scotland was entitled to rule the Church according to his pleasure. Six years prior to this, namely, on the 25th August, 1679, a woman called Janet Grant was tried for theft, in the baronial court of Sir Robert Gordon, of Gordonston, held at Drainie, and pleaded guilty. She was sentenced to be drowned next day in the Loch of Spynie.

In France, drowning was a capital punishment as late as 1793, but in Scotland we do not trace it later than 1685, and in England it was discontinued about the commencement of the seventeenth century.

Burning to Death.

BURNING to death was a frequent method of punishment in the barbarous days of many nations. In our own country it was used by the Anglo-Saxons as the penalty of certain crimes, and, as the ordinary punishment of witchcraft, it was maintained throughout the Middle Ages.

Burning alive was from early times the recognised method of uprooting heretical notions of religious belief of every class. The first to suffer from this cause in England was Alban, who died at the stake in the year A.D. 304. Since his day, thousands have suffered death on account of their religious belief, through intolerance; but that is not a subject we intend dealing with at the present time.

We desire to direct attention to some of the cases of the burning alive of women for civil offences. This practice was considered by the framers of the law as a commutation of the sentence of hanging, and a concession made to the sex of the offenders. "For as the decency due to the sex," says Blackstone, "forbids the exposing and publicly mangling their bodies, their sentence (which is to the full as terrible to sensation as the other) is, to be drawn to the gallows, and there to be burnt alive;" and he adds: "the humanity of the English nation has authorised, by a tacit consent, an almost general mitigation of such part of these judgments as savours of torture and cruelty, a sledge or hurdle being usually allowed to such traitors as are condemned to be drawn, and there being very few instances (and those accidental and by negligence) of any persons being disemboweled or burnt till previously deprived of sensation by strangling."

We gather from the annals of King's Lynn that, in the year 1515, a woman was burnt in the market-place for the murder of her husband. Twenty years later, a Dutchman was burnt for reputed heresy. In the same town, in 1590, Margaret Read was burnt for witchcraft. Eight years later, a woman was executed for witchcraft, and in the year 1616, another woman suffered death for the same crime. In 1791, at King's Lynn, the landlady of a public-house was murdered by a man let into the house at the dead of night by a servant girl. The man was hanged for committing the crime, and the girl was burnt at the stake for assisting the murderer to enter the dwelling.

There is an account of a burning at Lincoln, in 1722. Eleanor Elsom was condemned to death for the murder of her husband, and was ordered to be burnt at the stake. She was clothed in a cloth, "made like a shift," saturated with tar, and her limbs were also smeared with the same inflammable substance, while a tarred bonnet had been placed on her head. She was brought out of the prison bare-foot, and, being put on a hurdle, was drawn on a sledge to the place of execution near the gallows. Upon arrival, some time was passed in prayer, after which the executioner placed her on a tar barrel, a height of three feet, against the stake. A rope ran through a pulley in the stake, and was placed around her neck, she herself fixing it with her hands. Three irons also held her body to the stake, and the rope being pulled tight, the tar barrel was taken aside and the fire lighted. The details in the "Lincoln Date Book" state that she was probably quite dead before the fire reached her, as the executioner pulled upon the rope several times whilst the irons were being fixed. The body was seen amid the flames for nearly half-an-hour, though, through the dryness of the wood and the quantity of tar, the fire was exceedingly fierce.

An instance in which the negligence of the executioner caused death to be unnecessarily prolonged is found in the case of Catherine Hayes, who was executed at Tyburn, November 3rd, 1726, for the murder of her husband. She was being strangled in the accustomed manner, but the fire scorching the hands of the executioner, he relaxed the rope before she had become unconscious, and in spite of the efforts at once made to hasten combustion, she suffered for a considerable time the greatest agonies.

Two paragraphs, dealing with such cases, are in the *London Magazine* for July, 1735, and are as follow: "At the assizes, at Northampton, Mary Fawson was condemned to be burnt for poisoning her husband, and Elizabeth Wilson to be hanged for picking a farmer's pocket of thirty shillings."

"Among the persons capitally convicted at the assizes, at Chelmsford, are Herbert Hayns, one of Gregory's gang, who is to be hung in chains, and a woman, for poisoning her husband, is to be burnt."

In the next number of the same magazine, the first-mentioned criminal is again spoken of: "Mrs. Fawson was burnt at Northampton for poisoning her husband. Her behaviour in prison was with the utmost signs of contrition. She would not, to satisfy people's curiosity, be unveiled to anyone. She confessed the justice of her sentence, and died with great composure of mind." And also: "Margaret Onion was burnt at a stake at Chelmsford, for poisoning her husband. She was a poor, ignorant creature, and confessed the fact."

We obtain from Mr. John Glyde, jun., particulars of another case of burning for husband murder (styled petty treason). In April, 1763, Margery Beddingfield, and a farm servant, named Richard Ringe, her paramour, had murdered John Beddingfield, of Sternfield. The latter criminal was the actual murderer, his wife being considered an accomplice. He was condemned to be hanged and she burnt, at the same time and place, and her sentence was that she should "be taken from hence to the place from whence you came, and thence to the place of execution, on Saturday next, where you are to be burnt until you be dead: and the Lord have mercy on your soul." Accordingly, on the day appointed, she was taken to Rushmere Heath, near Ipswich, and there strangled and burnt. *

Coining was, until a late period, an offence which met with capital punishment. In May, 1777, a girl of little more than fourteen years of age had, at her master's command, concealed a number of whitewashed farthings to represent shillings, for which she was found guilty of treason, and sentenced to be burnt. Her master was already hanged, and the fagots but awaiting the application of the match to blaze in fury around her, when Lord Weymouth, who happened to be passing that way, humanely interfered. Said a writer in the *Quarterly Review*, "a mere accident saved the nation from this crime and this national disgrace."

In Harrison's *Derby and Nottingham Journal*, for September 23rd, 1779, is an account of two persons who were several days previously tried and convicted for high treason, the indictment being for coining shillings in Cold Bath Field, and for coining shillings in Nag's Head Yard, Bishopsgate Street. The culprit in the latter case was a man named John Fields, and in the former

* Glyde's "New Suffolk Garland," 1866.

a woman called Isabella Condon. They were sentenced to be drawn on a hurdle to the place of execution, the man to be hanged and the woman burnt.

Phœbe Harris, in 1786, was burnt in front of Newgate. The *Chelmsford Chronicle* of June 23rd, 1786, gives an account of her execution. After furnishing particulars of six men being hanged for various crimes, the report says:

"About a quarter of an hour after the platform had dropped, the female convicted" (Phœbe Harris, convicted of counterfeiting the coin called shillings) "was led by two officers of justice from Newgate to a stake fixed in the ground about midway between the scaffold and the pump. The stake was about eleven feet high, and, near the top of it was inserted a curved piece of iron, to which the end of the halter was tied. The prisoner stood on a low stool, which, after the ordinary had prayed with her a short time, being taken away, she was suspended by the neck (her feet being scarcely more than twelve or fourteen inches from the pavement). Soon after the signs of life had ceased, two cart-loads of fagots were placed round her and set on fire; the flames presently burning the halter, the convict fell a few inches, and was then sustained by an iron chain passed over her chest and affixed to the stake. Some scattered remains of the body were perceptible in the fire at half-past ten o'clock. The fire had not completely burnt out at twelve o'clock."

The latest instance on record is that of Christian Murphy, *alias* Bowman, who was burnt on March 18th, 1789, for coining.

The barbarous laws which permitted such repugnant exhibitions were repealed by the 30th George III., cap. 48, which provided that, after the 5th of June, 1790, women were to suffer hanging, as in the case of men.

Boiling to Death.

IN the year 1531, when Henry VIII. was king, an act was passed for boiling poisoners to death. The preamble of the statute states that one Richard Roose or Coke, a cook, by putting poison in some food intended for the household of the Bishop of Rochester, and for the poor of the parish in which his lordship's palace was situated in Lambeth Marsh, occasioned the death of a man and a woman, and the serious illness of several others. He was found guilty of treason, and sentenced to be boiled to death, without benefit of clergy, that is, that no abatement of the sentence was to be made on account of his ecclesiastical connection, nor to be allowed any indemnity such as was commonly the privilege of clerical offenders. He was publicly boiled to death at Smithfield, and the act ordained that all manner of poisoners should meet with the same doom henceforth.

A maid-servant, for poisoning her mistress, was, in 1531, boiled to death in the market-place of King's Lynn. Another instance of a servant poisoning the persons with whom she lived was Margaret Davy, who perished at Smithfield, in 1542.

This cruel law did not remain long on the Statute Books; shortly after the death of Henry VIII., and in the reign of the next king, Edward VI., it was, in 1547 repealed. The punishment of boiling alive was by no means uncommon before the enactment of Henry VIII., both in England and on the Continent.

Beheading.

BEHEADING, as a mode of punishment, had an early origin. Amongst the Romans it was regarded as a most honourable death. It is asserted that it was introduced into England from Normandy by William the Conqueror, and intended for the putting to death of criminals belonging to the higher grades of society. The first person to suffer beheading was Waltheof, Earl of Huntingdon, Northampton, and Northumberland, in 1076.

Since the days of the first Norman king down to the time of George the Second in 1747, two monarchs, and not a few of the most notable of the nobility of Great Britain, at the Tower, Whitehall, near the historic Tolbooth of Edinburgh, and other places have closed their noble, and in some instances ignoble, careers at the hands of the headsman.

Charles I. is perhaps the most famous of kings that have been beheaded. On January 30th, 1649, on a scaffold raised before the Banqueting House at Whitehall, he was executed. Within the Banqueting Hall of the Castle of Fotheringay, on February 8th, 1587, the executioner from the Tower, after three blows from an axe, severed the head from the body of Mary, Queen of Scots. Her earlier years opened in the gay court of France, and was full of sunshine, but shadows gathered, and she was—

> "A sad prisoner, passing weary years,
> In many castles, till at Fotheringay,
> The joyless life was ended."

Henry VIII. was a great king, but his cruel attitude towards his queens will ever diminish his glory; two of them were executed at his instigation at the Tower, namely, Anne Boleyn, on May 19th, 1536, and Katherine Howard, on February 13th, 1542. In the death at the block of Lady Jane Grey, "the nine days' queen," the scene is more pathetic and picturesque. On February 12th, 1553-4, she and her young husband, Lord Guildford Dudley, were executed at the Tower, the former on the Green within the ancient stronghold, and the latter on Tower Hill. The story of her unhappy fate is one of the most familiar pages of English history. Fuller said of this noble woman: "She had the innocency of childhood, the beauty of youth, the solidity of middle, the gravity of old age, and all at eighteen; the birth of a princess, the learning of a clerk, the

THE TOWER OF LONDON, SHOWING THE SITE OF THE SCAFFOLD.

life of a saint, and the death of a malefactor for her parents' offences."

Amongst the notable men who have suffered at

the Tower, we must mention John Fisher, Bishop of Rochester, beheaded on Tower Hill, June 23rd, 1535. He had nearly reached the age of four score years. The Pope, to spite Henry VIII., had sent the prelate a cardinal's hat, but the aged bishop had suffered death before it reached this country. Sir Thomas More was executed on July 6th, 1535. Like his friend Fisher, he refused submission to the Statute of Succession and to the King's Supremacy. The devotion of Margaret Roper to her father, Sir Thomas More, forms an attractive feature in the life story of this truly great man. After execution his head was spiked on London Bridge, and she bribed a man to move it, and drop it into a boat where she sat. She kept the sacred relic for many years, and at her death it was buried with her in a vault under St. Dunstan's Church, Canterbury.

George Boleyn, Viscount Rochford, was beheaded on May 17th, 1536, two days before the execution of his sister, Queen Anne Boleyn; and his wife, Jane, Viscountess Rochford, was beheaded at Tower Hill, with Katherine Howard, on February 13th, 1542, on the charge of having been an accomplice in the queen's treason. On July 28th, 1540, Thomas Cromwell, Earl of

Essex, was executed. Margaret Plantagenet, Countess of Salisbury, opposed the king and his government, and she was condemned for high treason. On May 27th, 1541, her earthly career closed. "The haughty old countess," it is recorded, "refused to lay her head upon the block, and the headsman had to follow her about the scaffold, and to 'fetch-off' her grey head 'slovenly' as he could."* She was nearly seventy years old.

The following are included in the list of notable men beheaded, and in most instances we are only able to give their names and dates of execution, but the story of their careers will be found in the pages of English history. Henry, Earl of Surrey, beheaded January 19th, 1546-7; Thomas, Lord Seymour of Sudeley, March 27th, 1548-9; Edward Seymour, Duke of Somerset, January 22nd, 1551-2; Sir Thomas Arundel, February 26th, 1551-2; John Dudley, Duke of Northumberland, August 22nd, 1553. Next comes Henry Grey, Duke of Suffolk, executed February 22nd, 1553-4. He was the father of Lady Jane Grey. Thomas Howard, Duke of Norfolk, suffered death June 2nd, 1572. On February

* Wilson's "The Tower and the Scaffold." 1879.

25th, 1600-1, Robert Devereux, Earl of Essex, was beheaded.

Sir Walter Raleigh was a many sided man, the discoverer of North Carolina, the defender of his country, an author, a court favourite, and a man of undaunted courage. In the Tower he was long a prisoner, and there wrote some notable books, and the following hymn :—

"Rise, O my soul, with thy desires to heav'n,
And with divinest contemplations use
Thy time, where time's eternity is given,
And let vain thoughts no more thy mind abuse;
But down in darkness let them lie;
So live thy better, let thy worse thoughts die.

"And thou, my soul, inspired with holy flame
View and review, with most regardful eye,
That holy cross, whence thy salvation came,
On which thy Saviour and thy sin did die;
For in that sacred object is much pleasure,
And in that Saviour, is my life, my treasure.

"To Thee, O Jesu, I direct my eye;
To Thee my hands, to Thee my humble knees,
To Thee my heart shall offer sacrifice,—
To Thee my thoughts, who my thoughts only sees;
To Thee myself, myself and all, I give;
To Thee I die, to Thee I only live."

On October 29th, 1618, Sir Walter Raleigh was executed at Whitehall under a sentence which had hung over his head for fifteen years.

On May 12th, 1641, was executed Wentworth, Earl of Strafford; and on January 10th, 1644-5, was beheaded Archbishop Laud. William Howard, Viscount Stafford, a victim of Oates's perjury, was executed on December 29th, 1680. "Having embraced and taken leave of his friends," says Bell, "he knelt down and placed his

AXE, BLOCK, AND EXECUTIONER'S MASK AT THE TOWER OF LONDON.

head on the block: the executioner raised the axe high in the air, but then checking himself suddenly lowered it. Stafford raised his head and asked the reason of the delay. The executioner said he waited the signal. 'I shall make no sign,' he answered, 'take your own time.' The executioner asked his forgiveness. 'I do forgive you,' replied Stafford, and placing his head again in position, at one blow it was severed from his body."*

A noted name in history comes next, the Duke of Monmouth. He was beheaded July 15th, 1685. "Here are six guineas for you," he said to the executioner, "and do not hack me as you did my Lord Russell. I have heard that you struck him three or four times. My servant will give you more gold if you do your work well." Then he undressed, felt the edge of the axe, and laid his head on the block. The executioner was unnerved, he raised his axe, but his arm trembled as it fell, and only a slight wound was inflicted. Several blows were given before the neck was severed.

We are now nearing the end of executions at the Tower, and only three more names occur. The cause of Prince Charlie was supported by not a few of the best blood of Scotland, but the battle of Culloden ended all hopes for the Pretender, and brought misery to many of his brave followers. William, Earl of Kilmarnock, and Arthur, Lord Balmerino, on August 18th, 1746,

* D. C. Bell's "Chapel of the Tower." 1877.

were beheaded for their devotion to the Jacobite cause. Simon, Lord Fraser of Lovat, had passed a shameless life, and little can be said in his favour.

LORD LOVAT (*from a drawing by Hogarth*).

In 1715, he fought against Prince Charles Edward, but subsequently joined the Jacobites, and took part in the battle of Culloden. He managed to escape from the field after the engagement, and it was not until April 9th, 1747, that he was beheaded on Tower Hill. On reaching the scaffold, he asked for the executioner, and presented him with a purse containing ten guineas. He then asked to see the axe, felt its edge, and said he thought it would do. Next he looked at his coffin, on which was inscribed :—

SIMON, DOMINUS FRASER DE LOVAT,
Decollat April 9, 1747,
Ætat suae 80.

After repeating some lines from Horace, and next from Ovid, he prayed, then bade adieu to his solicitor and agent in Scotland; finally the executioner completed his work, the head falling from the body. Lord Lovat was the last person beheaded in this country.

The Halifax Gibbet.

THE mention of the Halifax gibbet suggests a popular Yorkshire saying: "From Hell, Hull and Halifax, good Lord, deliver us." Fuller says the foregoing is part of the "Beggars' and Vagrants' Litany," and goes on to state: "Of these three frightful things unto them, it is to be feared that they least fear the first, conceiving it the farthest from them. Hull is terrible to them as a town of good government, where beggars meet with punitive charity; and, it is to be feared, are oftener corrected than amended. Halifax is formidable for the law thereof, whereby thieves, taken in the very act of stealing cloth, are instantly beheaded with an engine, without any further legal proceedings. Doubtless, the coincidence of the initial letters of these three words helped much the setting on foot of the proverb." The Halifax gibbet law has been traced back to a remote period. It has been suggested that it was imported into the country by some of the Norman barons. Holinshed's "Chronicle" (edition published in 1587) contains an interesting note bearing on this subject. "There is, and has been, of ancient time," says Holinshed, "a law or rather custom, at Halifax, that whosoever doth commit any felony, and is taken with the same, or confesses the fact upon examination, if it be valued by four constables to amount to the sum of thirteenpence-halfpenny, he is forthwith beheaded upon one of the next market-days (which fall usually upon the Tuesdays, Thursdays, and Saturdays), or else upon the same day that he is convicted, if market be holden. The engine wherewith the execution is done is a square block of wood, of the length of four feet and a half, which doth ride up and down in a slot, rabet, or regall, between two pieces of timber that are framed and set up right, of five yards in height. In the nether end of a sliding block is an axe, keyed or fastened with an iron into the wood, which, being drawn up to the top of the frame, is there fastened by a wooden pin (with a notch made in the same, after the manner of a Samson's post), unto the middest of which pin also there is a long rope fastened, that cometh down among the people; so that when the offender hath made his confession, and hath laid his neck over the nethermost block, every man there present doth either take hold of the rope (or putteth forth his arm so near to the same as he can get, in token that he is willing to see justice executed), and pulling out the pin in this manner, the head-block wherein the axe is fastened doth fall down with such a violence, that if the neck of the transgressor were so big as that of a bull, it should be cut in sunder at a stroke, and roll from the body by a huge distance. If it be so that the offender be apprehended for an ox, sheep, kine, horse, or any such cattle, the self beast or other of its kind shall have the end of the rope tied somewhere unto them, so that they, being driven, do draw out the pin, whereby the offender is executed."

In the illustration we give, which is a reproduction of an old picture, it will be observed that a horse is drawing the rope to loosen the pin, and to allow the axe to fall and cut off the head of the victim. The doomed man had doubtless stolen the horse. Near the gibbet are assembled the jurymen, and the parish priest is engaged in prayer.

Before a felon was condemned to suffer, the proof of certain facts appears to have been essentially necessary. In the first place, he was

HALIFAX GIBBET.

to be taken in the liberty of the forest of Hardwick, and if he escaped out of it, even after condemnation, he could not be brought back to be executed; but if he ever returned into the liberty again, and was taken, he was sure to suffer. It is recorded that a man named Lacy escaped, and resided seven years out of the forest, but returning, was beheaded on the former verdict. This person was not so wise as one Dinnis, who, having been condemned to die, escaped out of the liberty on the day fixed for his execution (which might be done by running in one direction about five hundred yards), and never returned. Meeting several people that asked if Dinnis was not to be beheaded on that day, his answer was, "I trow not," which, having some humour in it, became a proverbial saying in the district, and is used to this day—"'I trow not,' quoth Dinnis." In the next place, the fact was to be proved in the clearest manner. The offender had to be taken either hand-habend or back-berand, that is, having the stolen goods in his hand, or bearing them on his back, or, lastly, confessing that he took them.

The value of the goods stolen had to be worth at least thirteenpence-halfpenny, or more. Taylor, the water-poet, refers to the subject as follows :—

> "At Halifax the law so sharpe doth deale,
> That whoso more than thirteenpence doth steale,
> They have a jyn that wondrous quick and well
> Sends thieves all headless into heaven or hell."

A further condition of the Halifax gibbet law is scarcely so clear as the preceding. The accused was, after three market or meeting days, within the town of Halifax, next after his apprehension and being condemned, taken to the gibbet. This probably means that after he was delivered to the bailiff, no time further than was necessary was to elapse before proceeding to the trial, and that the bailiff was to send speedy summons to those who were to try him, which might be done in two or three days. If he were found guilty, the day of his execution depended upon that of his sentence, for he was to be beheaded on no other day than Saturday, which was the great meeting. Thus, if condemned on Monday, he would be kept three market days; but if condemned on Saturday, as some assert, he would be conducted straightway to the gibbet. The two last persons who suffered death by this engine were condemned and executed on the same day.

The final ordinance of the law directs that on

being led to the gibbet the malefactor is to have his head cut off from his body. That the machine was fully capable of this is evident both from Holinshed's remarks and from the following anecdote given by Wright, the historian of Halifax, as an extract from "A Tour through the Whole Island of Great Britain." A country woman, who was riding by the gibbet at the time of the execution of a criminal, had hampers at her sides, and the head, bounding to a considerable distance from the force of the descending axe, "jumped into one of the hampers, or, as others say, seized her apron with its teeth, and there stuck for some time."

The parish register at Halifax contains a list of forty-nine persons who suffered by the gibbet, commencing on the 20th day of March, 1541, the earliest date of which there is a recorded execution, and terminating on the 30th day of April, 1650. After which latter execution the bailiff of the town received an intimation that should another case occur, he would be called to public account. The number of beheadals in each of the reigns comprised in the above dates are : five in the last six years of the reign of Henry VIII. ; twenty-five in the reign of Elizabeth ; seven in the reign of James I.; ten in the reign of Charles I.; two during the Commonwealth.

In the year 1650, John Hoyle made a drawing of the Halifax gibbet, which is regarded as a faithful representation of it. On the crown of the hill will be noticed a sketch of the ancient beacon.

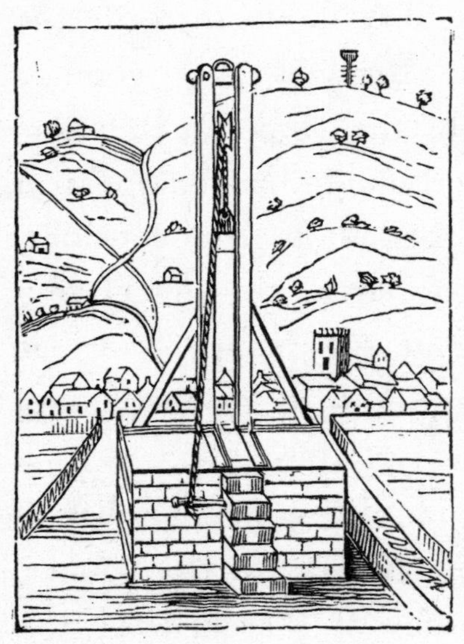

HALIFAX GIBBET, BY HOYLE.

An account of the last occasion upon which the services of the Halifax gibbet were called into requisition is interesting; it is contained in a rare book: "Halifax and its Gibbet Law placed in a True Light." It was written by Dr. Samuel Midgley, during an imprisonment for debt, and was published in 1708. "About the latter end of April, A.D. 1650, Abraham Wilkinson, John Wilkinson, and Anthony Mitchel were apprehended within the Manor of Wakefield and the liberties of Halifax, for divers felonious practices, and brought or caused to be brought into the custody of the chief bailiff of Halifax, in order to have their trials for acquittal or condemnation, according to the custom of the Forest of Hardwick, at the complaint and prosecution of Samuel Colbeck of Wardley, within the liberty of Halifax; John Fielden of Stansfield, within the said liberty; and John Cusforth of Durker, in the parish of Sandall, within the Manor of Wakefield." The Bailiff, according to the ancient custom, issued a summons to the "several constables of Halifax, Sowerby, Warley, and Skircoat," charging them to appear at his house on the 27th day of April, 1650, each accompanied by four men, "the most ancient, intelligent, and of the best ability" within his constabulary, to determine the cases. The constables were merely the law officers, the jurors being the sixteen "most ancient men," and whose names are given at length. They were empanneled in a convenient room at the Bailiff's house, where the accused and their prosecutors were brought "face to face" before them, as also the stolen goods, to be by them viewed, examined, and appraised. The court was opened by the following address from the Bailiff: "Neighbours and friends,—You are summoned hither and empanneled according to the ancient custom of the Forest of Hardwick, and by virtue you are required to make diligent search and inquiry into such complaints as are brought against the felons, concerning the goods that are set before you, and to make such just, equitable, and faithful determination betwixt party and party, as you will answer between God and your own conscience." He then addressed them on the separate charges against the prisoners. From Samuel Colbeck, of Warley, they were alleged to have stolen sixteen yards of russet-coloured kersey, which the jury valued at 1s. per yard. Two of the prisoners were alleged to have stolen from Durker Green, two colts, which were produced in court, one of which was appraised at £3, and the other at 48s. Also, Abraham Wilkinson was charged by John Fielden with stealing six yards of cinnamon-coloured kersey, and eight yards of white "frized, for blankets." After some debate concerning certain evidence against the above, and "after some mature consideration, the jury, as is customary in such cases," adjourned to the 30th day of April. Upon this day they met, and after further full examination gave their verdict in writing, and directed that the prisoners Abraham Wilkinson and Anthony Mitchel, "by ancient custom, and liberty of Halifax, whereof the memory of man is not to the contrary, the said Abraham Wilkinson and Anthony Mitchel are to suffer death by having their heads severed and cut off from their bodies at the Halifax gibbet, unto which verdict we subscribe our names." The felons were executed upon the same day.

The stone scaffold or pedestal upon which the gibbet was erected was discovered by the Town Trustees in 1840, in attempting to reduce what was known as Gibbet Hill to the level of the neighbouring ground; and except some decay of the top and one of the steps, it is in a perfect state. It is carefully fenced round, and an inscription affixed, which was done at the cost of Samuel Waterhouse, Mayor, in 1852. The gibbet axe, formerly in the possession of the Lord of the Manor of Wakefield, is now preserved at the Rolls Office of that town. It weighs seven pounds twelve ounces; its length is ten inches and a half; it is seven inches broad at the top, and nearly nine at the bottom, and at the centre about seven and a half.

The Scottish Maiden.

TOWARDS the middle of the sixteenth century, the Earl of Morton, Regent of Scotland, during a visit to England, witnessed an execution by the Halifax gibbet. He appears to have been impressed in a favourable manner with the ingenuity of the machine, and gave directions for a model of it to be made, and on his return home, in the year 1565, he had a similar gibbet constructed. On account of remaining so long before it was used, so runs the popular story, it was known as "The Maiden." Dr. Charles Rogers says that its appellation is from the Celtic *mod-dun*, originally signifying the place where justice was administered.* It is generally believed that the first victim beheaded at the Maiden was the Earl of Morton himself, but such was not the case, for he did not suffer death by it until June 2nd, 1581. He ruled Scotland for ten years, winning the approbation of Queen Elizabeth, but finally he fell a victim to the court faction. It has been said that probably it could not have availed

* Rogers's "Social Life in Scotland." 1884.

THE TOLBOOTH, EDINBURGH.

against him but for his own greed and cruelty. In trying to picture the scene of Morton's execution, says a painstaking author, it must have been a striking sight when the proud, stern, resolute face, which had frowned so many better men down, came to speak from the scaffold, protesting his innocence of the crime for which he had been condemned, but owning sins enough to justify God for his fate.* He died by the side of the City Cross, in the High Street, Edinburgh, and for the next twelve months his head garnished a pinnacle on the neighbouring Tolbooth.

THE SCOTTISH MAIDEN.

It is agreed by authorities that the first time the Maiden was used was at the execution of the inferior agents in the assassination of Rizzio, which

* Chambers's "Book of Days." Vol. I., page 728.

occurred at Holyrood Palace, on the 9th of March, 1566.

The list of those who have suffered death at the Maiden extends to at least one hundred and twenty names, not a few of whom Scotland

EXECUTION OF THE EARL OF ARGYLE.

delights to honour, including Sir John Gordon, of Haddo; President Spottiswood, the Marquis and the Earl of Argyle.

The unfortunate Earl of Argyle met his doom with firmness; when laying his head on the grim instrument of death, he said it was "a sweet Maiden, whose embrace would waft his soul into heaven." The tragic story of the Earl of Argyle has been ably told by Mr. David Maxwell, C.E., and his iniquitous death is one of many dark passages in the life of James II.*

In 1710, the use of the Maiden was discontinued. It now finds a place and attracts much attention in the Museum of the Society of Antiquaries of Scotland, at Edinburgh.

* David Maxwell's "Bygone Scotland," 1894.

Mutilation.

IN the earlier laws of England, mutilation or dismembering was by no means an uncommon punishment, more especially amongst the poor. Men, says Pike, branded on the forehead, without hands, without feet, without tongues, lived as an example of the danger which attended the commission of petty crimes, and as a warning to all men who had the misfortune of holding no higher position than that of a churl.* Wealthy people might do wrong with impunity. It has been clearly shown that there was one law for the rich, and another for the poor, in England during the four centuries which preceded the Norman Conquest.

According to Pike, under the Danes, mutilation was practised with perhaps greater severity than under the rule of the Saxons. Amongst the horrors of the Danish conquest were eyes plucked out; the nose, ears, and the upper lip were cut off; the scalp was torn away, and sometimes even, there is reason to believe, the whole body was flayed alive.

* Pike's "History of Crime in England." 1873.

Under the first two Norman kings mutilation of offenders was largely employed to preserve game in their forests. They, however, only appear to have enforced earlier laws. The earliest forest laws of which we have any knowledge are those which were promulgated about 1016 by Canute, the Dane, and probably much the same as had existed for a long period previously. The principal points of their tyrannical laws were, that if a freedman offered violence to a keeper of the King's deer, he was liable to lose his freedom and property; if a serf did the same, he lost his right hand; if the offence was repeated, he paid the penalty with his life. For killing a deer, either the eyes of the offender were put out, or he was killed; if anyone ran down a deer so that it panted, he was to pay at least ten shillings in the money of the day. Such was the law under the Saxon and the Danish Kings. The laws protected the private estate owner, and it was not until the Conqueror came that all the forest land was considered the property of the King.

In the reign of Henry I. coiners of false money were brought to Winchester and suffered there in one day the loss of their right hands and of their manhood. Under the Kings of the West Saxon dynasty the loss of the right hand was a common sentence for makers of base coin.

Several curious instances of mutilation are mentioned in "The Obsolete Punishments of Shropshire," by S. Meeson Morris. A case occurring in the reign of King John provides some interesting particulars. "In 1203," says Mr. Morris, "at the Salop Assizes, Alice Crithecreche and others were accused of murdering a woman at Lilleshall. Alice immediately, after the murder, had fled into Staffordshire with certain chattels of the murdered woman in her possession, and had been there arrested, and brought back into Shropshire. Her defence before the *Curia Comitatûs* of Salop was at least ingenious :—She alleged that on hearing a noise at night in the murdered woman's house she went and peeped through a chink in the door ; that she saw four men within, who presently coming out, seized, and threatened to murder her if she made any alarm, but on her keeping silence, gave her the stolen goods found upon her when arrested. On being brought before the Justices-in-Eyre at the above Assizes, Alice Crithecreche no longer adhered to this defence, and she was adjudged to deserve death, but the penalty was commuted for one hardly less terrible. It was ordered that both her eyes should be plucked out."

At a meeting of the Suffolk Institute of Archæology, held February 26th, 1889, Mr. George E. Crisp, of Playford Hall, near Ipswich, exhibited instruments used in the time of Henry VIII. for cutting off the ears, as a penalty for not attending Church.

In our chapter on the Pillory will be found particulars of cases of mutilation of the ears. The punishment of mutilation, except to the ears of the offender, was not common for centuries before the reign of Henry VIII., but by statute 33 Henry VIII., c. 12, the penalty for striking in the King's court or house was declared to be the loss of the right hand.*

* Morris's "Obsolete Punishments of Shropshire."

Branding.

THIS mode of punishment was discontinued in the reign of George III., and finally abolished in 1829. Old laws contain many allusions to the subject. In the reign of Edward VI. was passed the famous Statute of Vagabonds, authorising the branding with hot iron the letter V on the breast of a runaway slave. If, on being sold, he afterwards ran away, he might be branded on the cheek or forehead with the letter S, and thus the fact made known to those who saw him that he was a slave. Church brawlers in this reign were liable to be branded on the cheek with the letter F, meaning a fraymaker.

Gipsies were punished with branding. At Haddington, in 1636, some gipsies were severely dealt with, the men being condemned to be hanged, the women drowned, with the exception of those having children, and they were to be scourged through the burgh and burnt on their cheeks.

James Nayler, the Mad Quaker, who claimed to

be the Messiah, as part of his punishment for blasphemy, was condemned to have his tongue bored through and his forehead branded with a hot iron with the letter B, signifying that he was a blasphemer.*

Persons found guilty of petty offences and claiming benefit of clergy were burnt on the hand. Dr. Cox gives particulars of a case occurring at the Derbyshire Sessions in 1696. A butcher named Palmer, from Wirksworth, had been found guilty of stealing a sheep. He claimed benefit of clergy, which the court granted, and he read. The court gave judgment that he be burnt in his left hand, which was executed. His troubles did not end with the branding, for we find he had to "remaine in Gaole till hee finde Sufficient Suretyes for his Good behaviour to bee approved of and taken by Recoign by Mr. Justice Pole and Mr. Justice Borrowes, and for his appearance att next Sessions, and then to abide further Order of this Court." †

We reproduce from a carefully written work entitled, "In and Around Morecambe and Its

* Andrews's "Literary Byways." 1898.

† Cox's "Three Centuries of Derbyshire Annals." 1888.

Bay," issued by Mr. T. A. J. Waddington, York, an old time picture of a branding scene. In the Lancaster Criminal Court is still preserved a branding iron. "This iron," we are told, "is

"A FAIR MARK, MY LORD."

attached to the back part of the dock; it consists of a long bolt with a wooden handle at one end, and the letter M at the other. In close proximity are two iron loops designed for securing firmly the hand of the prisoner whilst the long piece of iron was heated red hot, so that the letter denoting 'Malefactor' could be impressed. The brander, after doing his fiery task, examined the hand, and on a good impression being made on the brawny part running from the thumb, would turn to the judge and exclaim—'A fair mark, my Lord!'"

At the Assizes held at Northampton, in 1720, before Mr. Justice Powis, the following prisoners were adjudged to be branded:—"Silvester Green, found guilty of sheep-stealing, burnt in the Hand. And James Corby, the Pig Merchant, had the Honour of the Brand confer'd on him likewise: Jane Clarke, William and John Green, convicted of several Petty Thefts and Larcenies, are to travel for 7 years after the proper Officer has kiss'd their Hand with a Red Hot Iron."

The foregoing list is drawn from the reports in the *Northampton Mercury*, and in the same paper for August 1st, 1721, it is stated "The following Persons were try'd at The Assizes held for The Town and County of Northampton, on Tuesday, the 26th of this Instant. Isabella Chapman and John Field were convicted of several Thefts and Larcenies. To be burnt in The Hand and whipt;

and afterwards to be transported for 7 years. Fielding's crime was stealing 12 sheep. . . . Isaac Emmerton, who was committed on the 21st May last . . . was burnt in The Hand."*

Branding in some instances appears to have been a mere farce. "When Charles Moritz, a young German, visited England in 1782, he was much surprised at this custom, and in his Diary he mentions that a clergyman had fought a duel with another in Hyde Park, and killed the man; he was found guilty of manslaughter, and was burnt in the hand, if that could be called burning which was done with a cold iron."* Such cases as this prepared the way for abolishing the custom, as cold irons for one class, and hot irons for another, could not be tolerated.

It was customary to command criminals in the courts in the past century to hold up their hands to prove if previous convictions had been passed upon them.

* Markham's "Ancient Punishments of Northamptonshire." 1886.

The Pillory.

IN the history of our own and other European countries, the pillory may be traced back to remote times, and its origin is almost lost in the mists of antiquity. Its story is one of tragedy and comedy, and full of historic interest and importance. In England, in bygone ages, the pillory was a familiar object, and perhaps no engine of punishment was more generally employed. Where there was a market, the pillory might be seen, for if the local authorities neglected to have it ready for immediate use, should occasion require it, they ran the risk of forfeiting the right of holding a market, which was a most serious matter in the olden time. Lords of Manors, in addition to having the right of a pillory, usually had a ducking-stool and gallows. Thomas de Chaworth, in the reign of Edward III., made a claim of a park, and the right of free warren, at Alfreton, with the privilege of having a gallows, tumbrel, and pillory.

In the middle ages frequently a pillory, whipping-post, and stocks were combined, and we give a picture of a good example from Wallingford, Berkshire. It will be observed that they are planned to hold four delinquents, namely, one in the pillory, one at the whipping-post, and two in the stocks. They stood near the town hall, in the market-place, down to about the year

PILLORY, WHIPPING-POST, AND STOCKS, WALLINGFORD.

1830, when the pillory and whipping-post were taken down. The stocks remained for a few years longer to remind the tippler of his fate, if he overstepped the bounds of temperance and was caught drunk. In course of time they fell into disuse, and were finally presented by the Corporation to Mr. J. Kirby Hedges, of Wallingford Castle, the historian of the ancient town. He informs us that there was a pillory at Wallingford in 1231, and probably earlier.

A good representation of the pillory formerly much used is furnished in a cut of Robert Ockam, undergoing part of his sentence for perjury, in the reign of Henry VIII.

In the year 1543, Ockam, with two other criminals mounted on horseback, with papers on their heads, and their faces towards the tails of the horses, had to ride about Windsor, Newbury, and Reading, and stand in the pillory of each of the three towns.

OCKAM IN THE PILLORY.

We give a view of an ancient pillory which formerly stood in the market-place of the village of Paulmy, in Touraine. It is copied from a picture of the Castle of Paulmy in *Cosmographie Universelle*, 1575. It will be observed that it is planned for holding a number of offenders at the same time. This form of pillory was not generally used. It was usually much simpler in construction, and frequently was not a permanent structure.

Stow, in his "Survey of London," supplies a description of the Cornhill pillory, and gives particulars of the crimes for which it was brought into requisition. After adverting to the making of a strong prison of timber, called a cage, and fixing upon it a pair of stocks for night-walkers, he next tells us: "On the top of the cage was placed a pillory, for the punishment of bakers offending in the assize of bread; for millers stealing of corn at the mill; for bawds, scolds, and other offenders." In the year 1468, the seventh of Edward IV., divers persons, being common jurors, such as at assizes were forsworn for rewards or favour of parties, and judged to

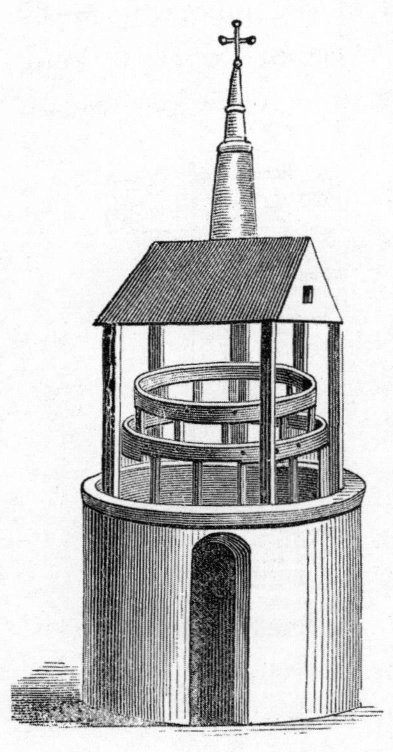

PILLORY FOR A NUMBER OF PERSONS.

ride from Newgate to the pillory of Cornhill, with mitres of paper on their heads, there to stand, and from thence again to Newgate; and this judgment was given by the Mayor of London. In the year 1509, the first of Henry VIII., Darby, Smith, and Simson, ringleaders of false inquests in London, rode about the city with their faces to horses' tails, and papers on their heads, and were set on the pillory in Cornhill, and afterwards brought again to Newgate, where they died for very shame, saith Robert Fabian.

A curious note, relating to this topic, appears in the "Journal of Henry Machyn, Citizen of London," published by the Camden Society. It is stated that, on the 1st July, 1552, there were a man and woman on the pillory in Cheapside; the man sold pots of strawberries, the which were not half full, but filled with fern. On the 30th May, 1554, two persons were set on the pillory, a man and woman; but the woman had her ears nailed to the pillory for speaking lies and uttering false rumours. The man was punished for seditious and slanderous words.

An instance of great severity is recorded in

1621, when Edward Floyde was convicted of having used slighting expressions concerning the king's son-in-law, the Elector Palatine, and his wife. The sentence was given as follows: (1) Not to bear arms as a gentleman, nor be a competent witness in any Court of Justice. (2) To ride with his face to a horse's tail, to stand in the pillory, and have his ears nailed, etc. (3) To be whipped at the cart's tail. (4) To be fined £5,000. (5) To be perpetually imprisoned in Newgate. It was questioned whether Floyde, being a gentleman, should be whipped, and have his ears nailed. It was agreed by a majority that he should be subject to the former, but not to the latter. He stood two hours in the pillory, and had his forehead branded.

Pepys, writing in his diary under date of March 26th, 1664, relates that he had been informed by Sir W. Batten that "some 'prentices, being put in the pillory to-day for beating of their masters, or such-like things, in Cheapside, a company of 'prentices came and rescued them, and pulled down the pillory; and they being set up again, did the like again." We may infer, from the foregoing and other facts that have come down to us respecting the London apprentices, that they were a power in bygone times, doing very much as they pleased.

We are enabled, by the courtesy of Messrs. W. & R. Chambers, to reproduce from their "Book of Days" an excellent illustration of Oates in the pillory (from a contemporary print). "Found guilty," says the writer in the "Book of Days," "of perjury on two separate indictments, the inventor of the Popish Plot was condemned, in 1685, to public exposure on three consecutive days. The first day's punishment, in Palace Yard, nearly cost the criminal his life; but his partisans mustered in such force in the city, on the succeeding day, that they were able to upset the pillory, and nearly succeeded in rescuing their idol from the hands of the authorities. According to his sentence, Oates was to stand every year of his life in the pillory, on five different days: before the gate of Westminster Hall, on the 9th August; at Charing Cross on the 10th; at the Temple on the 11th; at the Royal Exchange on the 2nd September; and at Tyburn on the 24th April; but, fortunately for the infamous creature, the Revolution deprived his determined enemies of power, and turned the criminal into a pensioner of Government."

It was formerly a common custom to put persons in the pillory during the time of public market. We may name, as an example, a case occurring at Canterbury, in 1524. A man was set up in the pillory, which was in the Market Place, and bearing on his head a paper inscribed, "This is a false, perjured, and forsworn man.' He was confined in the pillory until the market was over, and then led to Westgate and thrust out of the town, still wearing the paper. "If he be proud," says an old writer, "he may go home and shew himself among his neighbours."

The Corporation accounts of Newcastle-on-Tyne contain, among other curious items, the following:

1561.—Paid to the Gawyng Aydon, for squrgyn a boye about the town, and for settying a man in the pallerye, two days ... ... 16d.

1562.—Paid for a tre to the pillyre ... ... 5s.

1574.—Paid to Charles Shawe, for charges in carry-inge the man to Durham that stode in the pillarye, and was skrougide aboute the town at Mr. Maior's commandment... ... ... 3s

1593.—Paide for a Papist which studd in the pillerie for abusing Our Majestie by slanderous woordes... ... ... 14d.

1594.—Paid for 4 papers to 4 folke which was sett on the pillorie ... ... 16d.

Paid Ro. Musgrave for takinge paines to sett them upp ... ... 8d.

The "papers" above mentioned were for the purpose of proclaiming to the world at large the nature of the bearer's offence.

At Hull, in the year 1556, the town ordinances were revised and proclaimed "in the Market Place, in the market-time, according to the yearly custom." The twenty-third rule runs as follows: "That no person whomsoever presume to take down and carry away, any brick or stones off or from the town's walls, upon pain for every default to be set upon the pillory, and to pay, for a fine, to the town's chamber, forty shillings.' We may infer, from the foregoing, that the town's walls, both the original stone portion of Edward I., and the later addition of brick, were in a state of demolition. In 1559, the aldermen of Hull were directed to take account of "all vagabonds, idle persons, sharpers, beggars, and such like;" and, doubtless, not a few of the persons included under these wide definitions would come to the pillory, for the aldermen were ordered to "punish them severely;" and, as the punishments of Hull were largely in fines, Mr. Wildridge, author of "Old and New Hull," suggests that the moneyless classes of persons above-named would be most economically and severely dealt with by pillorying. About 1813, a man, for keeping a disreputable house, was placed in the pillory erected in the Market Place.

At Preston, Lancashire, in 1814, a man about sixty years of age was pilloried for a similar offence, and it is said that he was the last person punished in this manner in the town.

The pillory at Driffield was movable, and when in use stood in the Market Place, near the Cross Keys Hotel. The last occupants, a man and a woman, were pilloried together about 1810, for fortune-telling. At Bridlington the pillory stood in the Market Place, opposite the Corn Exchange. It was taken down about 1835, and lay some time in Well Lane, but it finally disappeared, and was probably chopped up for firewood. Before its removal there was affixed to it a bell, which was rung to regulate the market hours. Mischievous youths, however, often rang it, so it was taken down in 1810, and kept at a house down a court, known as Pillory Bell Yard.

Mr. W. E. A. Axon, the well known Lancashire author and antiquary, kindly furnishes us with particulars of the Manchester pillory. "The earliest notice of the pillory in Manchester," says Mr. Axon, "is in the Court Leet Records, April 8th, 1624, when the jury referred the erection of 'a gibbett' to the discretion of the Steward and the Boroughreeve. Some delay must have occurred, for on April 8th, 1625, 'the jurye doth order that the constables of this yeare, att the charges of the inhabitants, shall cause to bee

MANCHESTER PILLORY.

erected and sett vp a sufficient gibbett or pilorye for the vse of this towne, in some convenient place about the Markett Crosse, and to take to them the advice of Mr. Stewart and the Bororeve. This to be done before the xxiiijth day of

August next, subpena xx^s.' This threat of a penalty was effective, and the careful scribe notes *factum est*. The convenient place was in the market-place, close to the stocks. The pillory remained, more or less in use, until 1816, when it was removed. Barritt, the antiquary, made a drawing of it, which has been engraved. It was jocularly styled the 'tea table,' and was used as a whipping place also. In the present century, it was not a permanent fixture, but a movable structure, set up when required. One pilloried individual, grimly jesting at his own sorrows, told an inquiring friend that he was celebrating his nuptials with Miss Wood, and that his neighbour, whom the beadle was whipping, had come to dance at the wedding. During the Civil War, there was a pillory for the special benefit of the soldiers, and it was removed from the Corn Market in 1651."

The Rye pillory is still kept in the Town Hall, and we give a picture of it from a photograph. The last time it was used was in 1813, when a publican was put in it for aiding the escape of General Phillippon, a French prisoner of war, who had been brought to this old Sussex town. The pillory was erected on the beach, and the face of the culprit turned to the coast of France. Mr. Holloway, the local historian, supplied the late Mr. Llewellynn Jewitt with some particulars respecting this example. "It measures," says Mr. Holloway, "about six feet in height, by four in width. It consists of two up-posts affixed to a platform, and has two transverse rails, the upper one of which is divided horizontally, and has a hinge to admit of the higher portion being lifted, so as to allow of the introduction of the culprit's head and hands. Through the platform and the lower rail there are round perforations, into which, when the instrument was in requisition, an upright bar, probably of iron, was introduced, so as to allow the pillory, with its unfortunate tenant, to be turned bodily round at pleasure."

PILLORY AT RYE.

The famous Lord Thurlow was eloquent for the preservation of the pillory, which he called "the restraint against licentiousness, provided by the wisdom of past ages." This was in a case against the Rev. Horne Tooke, who, escaped with a fine of £200. Of others, who have spoken for and against it, may be mentioned Lord Macclesfield, who, in 1719, condemned it as a punishment for State criminals. In 1791, Pitt claimed to have dissuaded the Government from its too frequent use, as had Burke. Lord Ellenborough, in 1812, sentenced a blasphemer to the pillory for two hours once a month, for eighteen months. Again, in 1814, he ordered Lord Cochrane, the famous sea-fighter of Brasque Roads fame, to be pilloried for conspiring with others to spread false news. But his colleague, Sir Francis Burdett, declared that he would stand by his side in the pillory regardless of consequences. In the then state of public opinion, the Government declined to undertake the responsibility, and this punishment was waived.

It was no uncommon circumstance for the offenders to be killed on the pillory, by the pelting to which they were subjected by the fury of the crowd. In 1731, a professional witness, *i.e.*, one who, for the reward offered for the conviction of criminals, would swear falsely against them, was sentenced to the pillory of

Seven Dials, where so bitter were the populace against him that they pelted him to death. The coroner's jury returned a verdict of "wilful murder by persons unknown." In 1756, the drovers of Smithfield pelted two perjured thief-catchers so violently that one died; in 1763, a man died from a like cause, at Southwark; in 1780, a coachman died from injuries before his time had expired.

An amusing anecdote is related, bearing upon a pillory accident. "A man being condemned to the pillory in or about Elizabeth's time, the foot-board on which he was placed proved to be rotten, and down it fell, leaving him hanging by the neck, in danger of his life. On being liberated, he brought an action against the town for the insufficiency of its pillory, and recovered damages."*

In the year 1816, the pillory ceased to be employed for punishing persons, except in cases of perjury, and for this crime a man was put in the pillory in 1830. The pillory, in the year 1837, was abolished by Act of Parliament.

At the present time in China, the Cang, or Cangue is employed for punishing petty offenders.

* Chambers's "Book of Days."

From a picture we give from an original sketch recently made, it will be seen that it consists of a large wooden collar fitting close round the neck. The size and weight of the board varies, but it is not to be removed until the completion of the sentence, which may vary in length from a couple of weeks to three months. The name of the prisoner and the nature of his crime are written on the cang in large letters. He is left to public charity for support, and frequently suffers from the pangs of hunger.

THE CANG, CHINA.

Punishing Authors and Burning Books.

LITERARY annals contain many records of the punishments of authors. The Greeks and Romans frequently brought writers into contempt by publicly burning their books. In England, in years agone, it was a common practice to place in the pillory authors who presumed to write against the reigning monarch, or on political and religious subjects which were not in accord with the opinions of those in power. The public hangman was often directed to make bonfires of the works of offending authors. At Athens, the common crier was instructed to burn all the prohibited works of Pythagoras which could be found. It is well known that Numa Pompilius did much to build up the glory of Rome. It was he who gave to his countrymen the ceremonial laws of religion, and it was under his rule that they enjoyed the blessings of peace. His death was keenly felt by a grateful people, and he was honoured with a grand and costly funeral. In his grave were found some of his writings, which were contrary to his religious teaching; and the fact being made known to the Senate, an order was made directing the manuscripts to be consumed by fire. In the days of Augustus, no fewer than twenty thousand volumes were consigned on one occasion to the flames. The works of Labienus were amongst those which were burnt. It was a terrible blow to the author and some of his friends. Cassius Severus, when he heard the sentence pronounced, exclaimed in a loud voice that they must burn him also, for he had learnt all the books by heart. It was the death-blow to Labienus; he repaired to the tomb of his forefathers, refused food, and pined away. It is asserted that he was buried alive. At Constantinople, Leo I. caused two hundred thousand books to be consumed by fire.

The Bible did not escape the flames. It is stated by Eusebius that, by the direction of Dioletian, the Scriptures were burnt. According to Foxe, the well-known writer on the martyrs, on May, 1531, Bishop Stokesley "caused all the New Testament of Tindal's translation, and many other books which he had bought, to be openly burnt in St. Paul's churchyard." It was there that the Bishop of Rochester in a sermon denounced Martin Luther and all his works. He spoke of all who kept his books as accursed. Not a few of the condemned works were publicly burnt during the delivery of the sermon.

A man named Stubbs, in the reign of Queen Elizabeth, lost his hand for writing a pamphlet of Radical tendencies.

Collingbourne wrote the following couplet respecting Catesby, Ratcliff, and Lovel giving their advice to Richard III., whose crest, it will be remembered, was a white boar:

> "The cat, the rat, and Lovel the dog,
> Rule all England under a hog."

For writing the foregoing couplet, Collingbourne was executed on Tower Hill. After "having been hanged," it is recorded, "he was cut down immediately, and his entrails were then extracted and thrown into the fire; and all this was so speedily performed that," Stow says, "when the executioner pulled out his heart, he spoke, and said, 'Jesus, Jesus.'"

It is generally understood that Christopher Marlowe translated, as a college exercise, "Amores of Ovid." It was a work of unusual ability; but did not, however, meet with the approval of Archbishop Whitgift and Bishop Bancroft. In consequence, in June, 1599, all copies were ordered to be burnt. A few escaped the fire, and are now very valuable. Milton's books were burnt by the common hangman, on August 27th, 1659.

In 1630, Dr. Leighton, a clergyman, and father of the celebrated archbishop of that name, was tried and found guilty of printing a work entitled, "Zion's Plea against Prelacy," in which he called bishops men of blood, ravens, and magpies, and pronounced the institution of Episcopacy to be satanical; he called the Queen a daughter of Heth, and even commanded the murder of Buckingham. His sentence was a hard one, and consisted of a fine of £10,000. He was also degraded from the ministry, pilloried, branded, and whipped; an ear was cropped off, and his nostrils slit. After enduring these punishments, he was sent to the Fleet prison. At the end of the week, he underwent a second course of cruelty, and was consigned to prison for life. After eleven weary years passed in prison, Leighton was liberated, the House of Commons having reversed his sentence. He was told that his mutilation and imprisonment had been illegal! At that period in our history, a book or pamphlet could not be printed without a license from the

Archbishop of Canterbury, the Bishop of London, or the authorities of the two universities. Only authorised printers were permitted to set up printing presses in the city of London. Any one printing without the necessary authority subjected himself to the risk of being placed in the pillory and whipped through the City.

Lilburne and Warton disregarded the foregoing order, and printed and published libellous and seditious works. They refused to appear before the court where such offences were tried. The authorities found them guilty, and fined each man £500, and ordered them to be whipped from Fleet Prison to the pillory at Westminster. The sentence was carried out on April the 18th, 1638. Lilburne appears to have been a man of dauntless courage, and when in the pillory, he gave away copies of his obnoxious works to the crowd, and addressed them on the tyranny of his persecutors. He was gagged to stop his speech.

William Prynne lost his ears for writing "Histrio-Mastix: the Player's Scourge, or Actor's Tragedie" (1633.) His pillory experiences were of the most painful character.

According to an entry in the annals of Hull, in the year 1645, all the books of Common Prayer were burned by the Parliamentary soldiers, in the market-place.

One of the late Mr. C. H. Spurgeon's predecessors, named Benjamin Keach, a Baptist Minister, of Winslow, in the County of Bucks, issued a work entitled, "The Child's Instructor; or, a New and Easy Primmer." The book was regarded as seditious, and the authorities had him tried for writing and publishing it, at the Aylesbury Assizes, on the 8th October, 1664. The judge passed on him the following sentence:

"Benjamin Keach, you are here convicted of writing and publishing a seditious and scandalous Book, for which the Court's judgment is this, and the Court doth award, That you shall go to gaol for a fortnight, without bail or mainprise; and the next Saturday to stand upon the pillory at Ailsbury for the space of two hours, from eleven o'clock to one, with a Paper upon your head with this inscription, *For writing, printing and publishing a schismatical book, entitled, The Child's Instructor, or a new and easy Primmer.* And the next Thursday so stand in the same manner and for the same time in the market of Winslow; and there your book shall be openly burnt before your face by the common hangman, in disgrace to you and your doctrine. And you shall forfeit to the King's Majesty the sum of £20 and shall remain in gaol until you find sureties for your good behaviour and appearance at the next assizes, there to renounce your doctrine, and to make such public submission as shall be enjoined you."

We are told that Keach was kept a close

prisoner until the following Saturday, and on that day was carried to the pillory at Aylesbury, where he stood two hours without being permitted to speak to the spectators. It is recorded that his hands as well as his head were carefully kept in the pillory the whole time. The

BENJAMIN KEACH IN THE PILLORY.

next Thursday he stood in the same manner and length of time at Winslow, the town where he lived, and his book was burnt before him. "After this," we learn from Howell's "State Trials," "upon paying his fine, and giving sufficient security for his good behaviour, he was set at liberty; but was never brought to make recantation."

Defoe wrote much and well. He was by birth and education a Dissenter, and with much ability asserted the rights of Nonconformists. At a time when Churchmen were trying to obtain hard measures against the Dissenters, he directed against the Church party a severe satire, under the title of "The Shortest Way with the Dissenters." It exasperated the members of the Government, and a reward of fifty pounds was offered for his apprehension. The advertisement respecting him is a literary curiosity, and appeared in *The London Gazette*. It reads as follows:

"Whereas Daniel De Foe, *alias* De Fooe, is charged with writing a scandalous and seditious pamphlet, entitled, 'The Shortest Way with the Dissenters.' He is a middle-sized, spare man, about forty years old, of a brown complexion, and dark brown coloured hair, but wears a wig, a hooked nose, a sharp chin, grey eyes, and a large mole near his mouth; was born in London, and for many years was a hose factor, in Truman's-yard, in Cornhill, and now is owner of a brick and pantile works near Tilbury-fort, in Essex. Whoever shall discover the said Daniel De Foe to any of her Majesty's principal Secretaries of State, or any of Her Majesty's Justices of the Peace, so as he may be apprehended, shall have a reward of fifty pounds, which Her Majesty has ordered immediately to be paid upon such discovery."

He managed to keep out of the way of the

authorities, but on hearing that the printer and publisher of the pamphlet were put into prison, he gave himself up, and they were set at liberty. Defoe was tried at the Old Bailey, in July, 1704, and pleaded guilty. It is said that he put in this plea on the promise of pardon secretly given to him. He did not, however, escape punishment; he was fined two hundred marks, and ordered to appear three times in the pillory, and remain in prison during the Queen's pleasure.

During his imprisonment before being placed in the pillory, he wrote the famous "Hymn to the Pillory," which was speedily put into type and sung by the crowd at the time Defoe was in the machine. Here are some lines from it:

Hail hieroglyphic State machine,
Contrived to punish fancy in:
Men that are men in thee can feel no pain,
And all thy insignificants disdain;
Contempt, that false new word for shame,
Is, without crime, an empty name;
A shadow to amuse mankind,
But ne'er to fright the wise or well-fixed mind.
Virtue despises human scorn!

. . . .

Even learned Selden saw
A prospect of thee through the law.
He had thy lofty pinnacles in view,
But so much honour never was thy due.

The first intent of laws
Was to correct the effect, and check the cause,
And all the ends of punishment
Were only future mischiefs to prevent.
But justice is interverted when
Those engines of the law,
Instead of pinching vicious men,
Keep honest ones in awe.

. . . .

Tell them the men that placed him there
Are friends unto the times;
But at a loss to find his guilt,
And can't commit his crimes.

Defoe fared well in the pillory. He was not pelted with rotten eggs, but with flowers; and beautiful garlands were suspended from the pillory. In a modest manner, he gave an account of the affair. "The people," he wrote, "were expected to treat me very ill, but it was not so. On the contrary, they were with me—wished those who had set me there were placed in my room, and expressed their affections by loud thanks and acclamations when I was taken down."

There is not the least truth in Pope's well-known, and we may say disgraceful line:

Earless, on high stood unabash'd De Foe.

After Defoe had spent about a year in prison, the Queen sent to his wife money to pay the fine.

A work was issued in 1704, entitled, "The

Superiority and Dominion of the Crown of England over the Crown of Scotland," by William Attwood. The Scottish Parliament had the publication under consideration, and pronounced it scurrilous and full of falsehoods, and finally commanded the public hangman of Edinburgh to burn the book.

Williams, the bookseller, was put in the pillory in the year 1765, for republishing the *North Briton* in forty-five volumes. "The coach," says *The Gentleman's Magazine*, "that carried him from the King's Bench Prison to the pillory was No. 45. He was received with the acclamations of a prodigious concourse of people. Opposite to the pillory were erected two ladders, with cords running from each other, on which were hung a jack-boot, an axe, and a Scotch bonnet. The latter, after remaining some time, was burnt, and the top-boot chopped off. During his standing, also, a purple purse, ornamented with ribbands of an orange colour, was produced by a gentleman, who began a collection in favour of the culprit by putting a guinea into it himself, after which, the purse being carried round, many contributed, to the amount in the whole, as supposed, of about two hundred guineas." The spectators loudly cheered Mr. Williams on getting into and out of the pillory. He held a sprig of laurel in his hand during the time he was confined in the pillory.

Alexander Wilson, the famous ornithologist and poet, in the year 1793, was tried for publishing some satirical poems concerning certain Paisley manufacturers. The pieces were regarded as libellous, and he was fined £12 13s. 6d., and condemned to burn in a public manner his poems at the Market Cross at Paisley. The poet was unable to pay the fine, and had to go to prison for a short time. The circumstance was the chief cause of Wilson leaving Scotland for America.

Finger Pillory.

FINGER PILLORIES, or stocks, in past ages, were probably frequently employed in the old manorial halls of England; but at the present period only traces of a few are to be found. The most interesting example is one in the parish church of Ashby-de-la-Zouch, Leicestershire, which has been frequently described and illustrated. An account of it appears in *Notes and Queries* of October 25th, 1851. It is described as "fastened at its right hand extremity into a wall, and consists of two pieces of oak; the bottom and fixed piece is three feet eight inches long; the width of the whole is four-and-a-half inches, and when closed, it is five inches deep: the left hand extremity is supported by a leg of the same width as the top, and two feet six inches in length; the upper piece is joined to the lower by a hinge, and in this lower and fixed horizontal part are a number of holes, varying in size; the largest are towards the right hand: these holes are sufficiently deep to admit the finger to the second joint, and a slight hollow is made to admit the third one, which lies flat; there is, of course, a corresponding hollow at the top of the moveable part, which, when shut down, encloses the whole finger." Thomas Wright, F.S.A., in his "Archæological Album," gives an illustration of the Ashby-de-la-Zouch example, and we reproduce a copy. It shows the manner in which the finger was confined, and it will easily be seen that it could not be withdrawn until the pillory was opened. If the offender were held long in this posture, the punishment must have been extremely painful.

FINGER-PILLORY, ASHBY-DE-LA-ZOUCH.

Amongst the old-time relics at Littlecote Hall, an ancient Wiltshire mansion, may still be seen a finger-pillory. It is made of oak. We give an illustration of it from a drawing executed expressly for this work. At Littlecote Hall it is spoken of as an instrument of domestic punishment.

Plot, in his "History of Staffordshire," published in 1686, gives an illustration of one of these old-time finger-pillories. "I cannot forget," writes Plot, "a piece of art that I found in the Hall of the Right Honourable William Lord Paget, at Beaudesart, made for the punishment of disorders that sometimes attend feasting, in

FINGER-PILLORY, LITTLECOTE HALL.

Christmas time, etc., called the finger-stocks, into which the Lord of Misrule used to put the fingers of all such persons as committed misdemeanours, or broke such rules as, by consent, were agreed on for the time of keeping Christmas among the servants and others of promiscuous quality ; these being divided in like manner as the stocks of the legs, and having holes of different sizes to fit for scantlings of all fingers, as represented in the table." We reproduce a sketch of Plot's picture.

In an account of the Customs of the Manor of Ashton-under-Lyne, in the fifteenth century, it is stated at the manorial festivals, "in order to preserve as much as possible the degree of decorum that was necessary, there were frequently

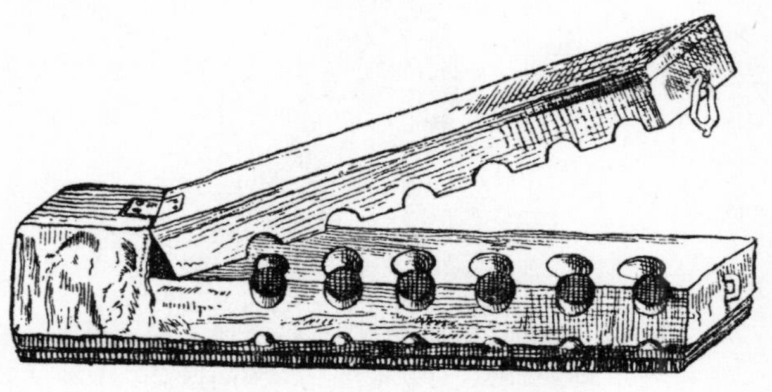

FINGER-PILLORY, BEAUDESART.

introduced a diminutive pair of stone stocks of about eighteen inches in length, for confining within them the fingers of the unruly."

In connection with this chapter may be fitly included a picture of a finger-pillory in the possession of Mr. England Howlett, Kirton-in-Lindsey, Lincolnshire. Our illustration is half the size of the original implement represented, which is from a Welsh village. This ingenious contrivance was used until the early part of this century. It was kept on the dame's desk, and when the children went up to say their lessons they had to place their hands behind them, putting their fingers into the holes of the pillory,

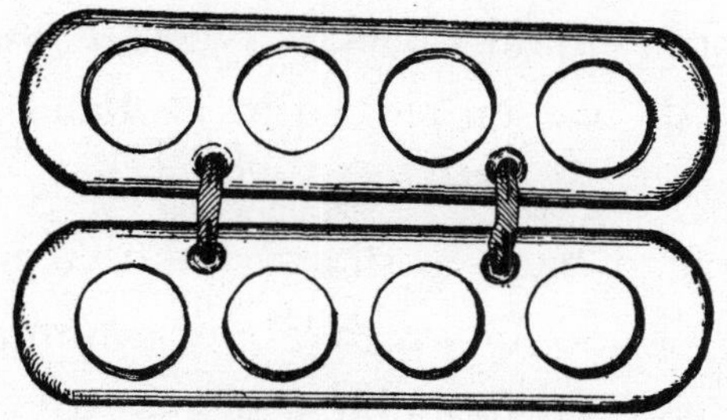

FINGER-PILLORY FROM AN OLD DAME'S SCHOOL.

and bringing their hands back to back. When properly fixed, the hands were quite fast and the shoulders held well back. This kind of finger-pillory was frequently used as a means of punishment in schools.

The Jougs.

THIS old-time instrument of punishment was more generally used in North Britain than in England. It was employed in Holland, and most likely in other countries. In Scotland, its history may be traced back to the sixteenth century, and from that period down to about a hundred years ago, it was a popular means of enforcing ecclesiastical discipline, and was also brought into requisition for punishing persons guilty of the lesser civil offences. In Scotland the jougs were usually fastened to a church door, a tree in a churchyard, the post of a church gate, a market cross, or a market tron, or weighing-post, and not infrequently to prison doors.

The jougs are simple in form, consisting of an iron ring or collar, with a joint or hinge at the back to permit its being opened and closed, and in the front are loops for the affixing of a padlock to secure it round the neck of the culprit.

The "Diary of Henry Machyn, Citizen and Merchant-Taylor of London, from A.D. 1550 to

A.D. 1563" (published by the Camden Society in 1848), contains the following note on the use of the jougs: "The 30th day of June, 1553," it is stated, "was set a post hard by the Standard in Cheap, and a young fellow tied to the post with a collar of iron about his neck, and another to the post with a chain, and two men with two whips whipping them about the post, for pretended visions and opprobrious and seditious words." We have modernised the spelling of Machyn.

Disregarding parental authority in Scotland was frequently the cause of young folk being punished by the jougs, and in other ways. Harsh rules of life were by no means confined to North Britain. In Tudor England manners were severe and formal, parents exacting abject deference from their offspring. A child did not presume to speak or sit down without leave in presence of its parents. A little leniency was extended to girls, for when tired they might kneel on cushions at the far end of the room; but boys were expected to stand with their heads uncovered. It is to be feared that true domestic bliss was almost unknown in olden times. Teachers were equally tyrannical, and it is a matter of history that Roger Ascham, the tutor of Queen Elizabeth, used to "pinch, nip, and bob [slap] the princess when she displeased him."

Some very curious facts relating to this subject appear in the old Kirk-Session records. "David Leyes, who struck his father," was, by a Kirk-Session of St. Andrews, in 1574, sentenced to appear before the congregation "bairheddit and beirfuttit, upon the highest degree of the penitent stuool, with a hammer in the ane hand and ane stane in the uther hand, as the twa instruments he mannesit his father,—with ane papir writin in great letteris about his heid with these wordis, 'Behold the onnaturall Son, punished for putting hand on his father, and dishonouring of God in him.'" Nor was this deemed sufficient humiliation, for the offender was afterwards made to stand at the market cross two hours "in the jaggs, and thereafter cartit through the haill toun." It was also resolved that "if ever he offended father or mother heireafter, the member of his body quhairby he offendit sal be cuttit off from him, be it tung, hand or futt without mercy, as examples to utheris to abstein fra the lyke." At Glasgow, in the year 1598, the Presbytery carefully considered the conduct of a youth who had passed his father "without lifting his bonnet,"

A servant in Wigtown, in 1649, was brought before the magistrates for raising her hand and abusing her mistress, and was ordered to stand a full hour with the jougs round her neck.

At Rothesay, a woman gave the members of the Kirk-Session a great deal of trouble through departing from the path of sobriety. Persuasion and rebuke were tried without avail. At last, in the year 1661, the Session warned her that "if hereafter she should be found drunk, she would be put in the jouggs and have her dittay written on her face."*

Mr. James S. Thomson read a paper before the Dumfries Antiquarian Society, supplying some interesting glimpses of bygone times, furnished by the Kirk-Session Records of Dumfries. Not the least important information was that relating to punishments of the past. It will not be without interest to notice a few of the cases. In the year 1637, a man named Thomas Meik had been found guilty of slandering Agnes Fleming, and he was sentenced to stand for a certain time in the jougs at the tron, and subsequently on his bare knees at the market cross to ask her pardon.

The case of Bessie Black was investigated, and

* Rogers's "Scotland, Social and Domestic."

it was proved that for the third time she had been found guilty of leaving the path of virtue, and for her transgressions she was directed for six Sabbaths to stand at the Cross in the jougs. In another case it was proved that two servants had been found guilty of scolding each other, and sentence was given that they were "to be put into the jougs presently." A curious sentence was passed in the year 1644. A man and his wife were ordered to stand at the Kirk-style with the branks in their mouths.

Exposure of persons to the contempt of the public was formerly a common form of punishment in Scotland. Curious information bearing on the subject may be gleaned from the old newspapers. We gather from the columns of the *Aberdeen Journal*, for the year 1759, particulars of three women, named Janet Shinney, Margaret Barrack, and Mary Duncan, who suffered by being exposed in public. "Upon trial," it is reported, "they were convicted, by their own confessions, of being in the practice, for some time past, of stealing and resetting tea and sugar, and several other kinds of merchant's goods, from a merchant in the town. And the Magistrates have sentenced them to be carried to the Market

Cross of Aberdeen, on Thursday the 31st [May, 1759], at twelve o'clock at noon, and to be tied to a stake bareheaded for one hour by the executioner, with a rope about each of their necks, and a paper on their breasts denoting their crime; to be removed to prison, and taken down again on Friday the 1st June at twelve o'clock, and to stand an hour at the Market Cross in the manner above mentioned; and thereafter to be transported through the whole streets of the town in a cart bareheaded (for the greater ignominy), with the executioner and tuck of drum, and to be banished the burgh and liberties in all time coming." In bygone ages, it was a common custom to banish persons from towns for immoral conduct. A woman at Dumfries, for

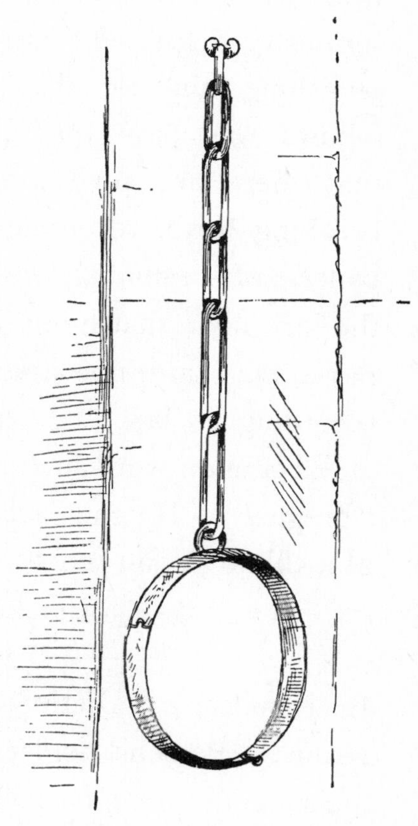

THE JOUGS, PRIORY CHURCH, BRIDLINGTON.

example, was for a fourth lapse from virtue sentenced "to be carted from the toun."

At a meeting of the Kirk-Session at Lesmahagow, held in June, 1697, the case of a shepherd who had shorn his sheep on the Parish Fast was seriously discussed, with a view to severely punishing him for the offence. A minute as follows was passed: "The Session, considering that there are several scandals of this nature breaking forth, recommends to the bailie of the bailerie of Lesmahagow to fix a pair of jougs at the kirk door, that he may cause punish corporally those who are not able to pay fines, and that according to law."

A common word in Ayrshire for the jougs was "bregan." In the accounts of the parish of Mauchline is an entry as under:

1681. For a lock to the bregan and mending it £1 16 0

In Jamieson's "Dictionary" it is spelled "braidyeane." Persons neglecting to attend church on the Sunday were frequently put into the jougs. Several cases of this kind might be cited, but perhaps particulars of one will be sufficient. A man named John Persene was brought before the Kirk-Session of Galston, in 1651. He admitted he had not been to church for the space of five weeks. For thus neglecting to attend to the ordinances, he was "injoyned to apier in the public place of repentence, and there to be publicly rebuked, with certificatione that if he be found to be two Sabbaths together absent from the church he shall be put in the breggan."

In "Prehistoric Annals of Scotland," by Daniel Wilson, LL.D. (London, 1863), there is a drawing of a fine old pair of jougs, "found," says Wilson, "imbedded in a venerable ash tree, recently blown down, at the churchyard gate, Applegirth, Dumfriesshire. The tree, which was of great girth, is believed to have been upwards of three hundred years old, and the jougs were completely imbedded in its trunk, while the chain and staple hung down within the decayed and hollow core." The jougs belonging to the parish of Galashiels are preserved at Abbotsford. At Merton, Berwickshire, the jougs may be seen at the church. The Fenwick jougs are still fastened to the church wall, and the old Session Records of the parish contain references to cases where persons were ordered to "stand in the jougs from eight till ten, and thence go to the place of repentence within ye kirk." At the village of Kilmaurs,

Ayrshire, the jougs are attached to the old Tolbooth, at the town of Kinross are fastened to the market cross, and at Sanquhar they are in front of the town hall.

We give three illustrations of the jougs. One represents a very fine example, which may be seen in the Priory Church of Bridlington, Yorkshire.

JOUGS FROM THE OLD CHURCH OF CLOVA, FORFARSHIRE.

We believe that this is the first picture which has been published of this interesting old-times relic. It is referred to in the local guide book, but no information is given as to when last used.

It is stated in the "History of Wakefield Cathedral," by John W. Walker, F.S.A., that "an old chain, leaded into the wall at the junction of the north aisle with the tower in the interior of the church, is said to have been used for the purpose of fastening up persons who disturbed the service." This may be safely assumed that formerly the jougs were affixed at the end of the chain.

In the Museum of the Society of Antiquaries of Scotland, Edinburgh, may be seen the jougs of

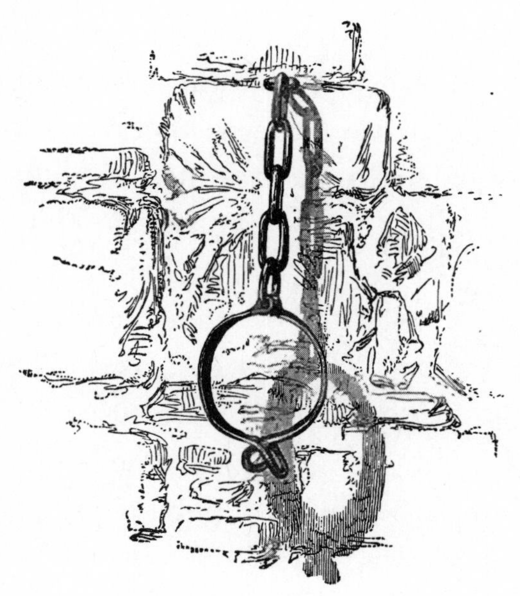

THE JOUGS AT DUDDINGSTON.

the old parish church of Clova, Forfarshire. About a mile from Edinburgh is the charming hamlet of Duddingston, and at the churchyard gate are the jougs, which form a curious link between the ruder customs of bygone ages and the more refined life of modern times.

The Stocks.

STOCKS were used, at an early period, as a means of punishing breakers of the law. The precise date when they were first employed in this country is not known, but we may infer from early mediæval illustrations that the stocks were in general use amongst the Anglo-Saxons, for they often figure in drawings of their public places. The picture we here give is from the Harleian MSS., No. 65. The stocks were usually placed by the side of the public road, at the entrance of a town. It will be observed that two offenders are fastened to the columns of a public building by means of a rope or chain. It has been suggested that it is a court-house.

ANGLO-SAXON PUNISHMENTS.

The "Cambridge Trinity College Psalter"—an illuminated manuscript—presents some curious illustrations of the manners of the earlier half of the twelfth century. We give a reproduction of one of its quaint pictures. Two men are in the stocks; one, it will be seen, is held by one leg only, and the other by both, and a couple of persons are taunting them in their time of trouble.

Stocks were not only used as a mode of punishment, but as means of securing offenders. In bygone times, every vill of common right was compelled to erect a pair of stocks at its own expense. The constable by common law might

TAUNTING PERSONS IN THE STOCKS.

place persons in the stocks to keep them in hold, but not by way of punishment.

We gather from an Act passed during the reign of Edward III., in the year 1351, and known as the Second Statute of Labourers, that if artificers were unruly they were liable to be placed in the stocks. Some years later, namely, in 1376, the Commons prayed that the stocks might be established in every village. In 1405, an Act was passed for every town and village to be provided with a pair of stocks, so that a place which had not this instrument of punishment and detention was regarded as a hamlet. No village was considered to be complete, or even worthy of the name of village, without its stocks, so essential to due order and government were they deemed to be. A Shropshire historian, speaking of a hamlet called Hulston, in the township of Middle, in order, apparently, to prove that in calling the place a hamlet and not a village he was speaking correctly, remarks in proof of his assertion, that Hulston did not then, or ever before, possess a constable, a pound, or stocks.*

Wynkyn de Worde, who, in company with Richard Pynsent, succeeded to Caxton's printing business, in the year 1491, issued from his press the play of "Hick Scorner," and in one of the scenes the stocks are introduced. The works of Shakespeare include numerous allusions to this subject. Launce, in "The Two Gentlemen of Verona" (IV. 4), says: "I have sat in the stocks for puddings he hath stolen." In "All's Well that Ends Well" (IV. 3), Bertram says: "Come, bring forth this counterfeit module has deceived me, like a double-meaning prophesier." Whereupon one

* Morris's "Obsolete Punishments of Shropshire."

of the French lords adds: "Bring him forth; has sat i' stocks all night, poor gallant knave." Volumnia says of Coriolanus (V. 3):

> "There's no man in the world
> More bound to's mother; yet here let me prate
> Like one i' the stocks."

Again, in the "Comedy of Errors" (III. 1), Luce speaks of "a pair of stocks in the town," and in "King Lear" (II. 2), Cornwall, referring to Kent, says:

> "Fetch forth the stocks!
> You stubborn ancient knave."

It would seem that formerly, in great houses, as in some colleges, there were movable stocks for the correction of the servants.*

In Butler's "Hudibras" are allusions to the stocks. Says the poet:

> "An old dull sot, who toll'd the clock
> For many years at Bridewell-dock;
>
> . . . . . .
>
> "Engaged the constable to seize
> All those that would not break the peace;
> Let out the stocks and whipping-post,
> And cage, to those that gave him most."

We are enabled, by the kindness of Mr. Austin Dobson, author of "Thomas Bewick and his

* Dyer's "Folk-Lore of Shakespeare."

Pupils," to reproduce from that work a picture of the stocks, engraved by Charlton Nesbit for Butler's "Hudibras," 1811.

Scottish history contains allusions to the stocks; but in North Britain they do not appear to have been so generally used as in England. On the 24th August, 1623, a case occupied the attention of the members of the Kirk-Session of

IN THE STOCKS, BY NESBIT.

Kinghorn. It was proved that a man named William Allan had been guilty of abusing his wife on the Sabbath, and for the offence was condemned to be placed twenty-four hours in the stocks, and subsequently to stand in the jougs two hours on a market day. It was further intimated to him that if he again abused his wife, he would be banished from the town. We give a picture of the stocks formerly in the Canongate Tolbooth, Edinburgh, and now in the Scottish Antiquarian Museum.

It was enacted, in the year 1605, that every person convicted of drunkenness should be fined five shillings or spend six hours in the stocks, and James I., in the year 1623, confirmed the Act. Stocks were usually employed for punishing drunkards, but drunkenness was by no means the

STOCKS FROM THE CANONGATE TOLBOOTH.

only offence for which they were brought into requisition. Wood-stealers, or, as they were styled, "hedge-tearers," were, about 1584, set in the stocks two days in the open street, with the stolen wood before them, as a punishment for a second offence.* Vagrants were in former times often put in the stocks, and Canning's "Needy Knife-Grinder" was taken for one, and punished.

In a valuable work mainly dealing with

* Roberts's "Social History of the Southern Counties of England." 1856.

Devonshire, by A. H. A. Hamilton, entitled, "Quarter Sessions from Queen Elizabeth to Queen Anne," there is an important note on this subject. "A favourite punishment," says Hamilton, "for small offences, such as resisting a constable, was the stocks. The offender had to come into the church at morning prayer, and say publicly that he was sorry, and was then set in the stocks until the end of the evening prayer. The punishment was generally repeated on the next market day."

Tippling on a Sunday during public divine service was in years agone a violation of the laws, and frequently was the means of offenders being placed in the stocks. In Sheffield, from a record dated February 12th, 1790, we find that for drinking in a public-house, during the time of service in the church, nine men were locked in the stocks. "Two boys," we find it is stated in the same work, "were made to do penance in the church for playing at trip during divine service, by standing in the midst of the church with their trip sticks erect."

Not far distant from Sheffield is the village of Whiston, and here remain the old parish stocks near to the church, and bear the date of 1786.

Perhaps the most notable person ever placed in the stocks for drinking freely, but not wisely, was Cardinal Wolsey. He was, about the year 1500, the incumbent at Lymington, near Yeovil, and at the village feast had overstepped the bounds of moderation, and his condition being made known to Sir Amias Poulett, J.P., a strict moralist, he was, by his instructions, humiliated by being placed in the stocks. It was the general practice in bygone days, not very far remote, for church-wardens to visit the various public-houses during the time of church service and see that no persons were drinking. At Beverley, about 1853, the representatives of the church, while on their rounds, met in the streets a well-known local character called Jim Brigham, staggering along the street. The poor fellow was taken into custody, and next day brought before the Mayor, and after being severely spoken to about the sin of Sunday tippling, he was sentenced to the stocks for two hours. An eye-witness to Jim's punishment says: "While he was in the stocks, one of the Corporation officials placed in Jim's hat a sheet of paper, stating the cause of his punishment and its extent. A young man who had been articled to a lawyer, but who was not practising, stepped forward, and taking the paper out, tore it into shreds, remarking it was no part of Jim's sentence to be subjected to that additional disgrace. The act was applauded by the on-lookers. One working-man who sympathised with him, filled and lit a tobacco pipe, and placed it in Jim's mouth; but it was instantly removed by one of the constables, who considered it was a most flagrant act, and one calling for prompt interference on the part of the guardians of the law." Brigham was the last person punished in the stocks at Beverley. The stocks, which bear the date 1789, were movable, and fitted into sockets near the Market Cross. They are still preserved in a chamber at St. Mary's in that town. The Minster, Beverley, had also its stocks, which are still preserved in the roof of that splendid edifice.

The stocks were last used at Market Drayton about sixty years ago. "It is related," says Mr. Morris, "that some men, for imbibing too freely and speaking unseemly language to parishioners, as they were going to church on a Sunday morning, were, on the following day, duly charged with the offence and fined, the alternative being confinement for four hours in the stocks. Two of the men refused to pay the fine, and were consequently put therein. The people flocked around them, and, while some regaled them with an ample supply of beer, others expressed their sympathy in a more practical way by giving them money, so that, when released, their heads and their pockets were considerably heavier than they had been on the previous Sunday." At Ellesmere, the stocks, whipping-post, and pillory were a combination of engines of punishment. The former were frequently in use for the correction of drunkards. A regular customer, we read, was "honoured by a local poet with some impromptu verses not unworthy of reproduction :

'A tailor here ! confined in stocks,
  A prison made of wood—a—,
Weeping and wailing to get out,
  But couldna' for his blood—a—
The pillory, it hung o'er his head,
  The whipping-post so near—a—
A crowd of people round about
  Did at William laugh and jeer—a—'"

"The style was," it is said, "a sarcastic imitation of 'William's' peculiar manner of speaking when tipsy."

According to Mr. Christopher A. Markham, in his notices of Gretton stocks, they "still stand on the village green; they were made to secure three men, and have shackles on the post for whipping; they are in a good state of repair. Joshua Pollard, of Gretton, was placed in them, in the year 1857, for six hours, in default of paying five shillings and costs for drunkenness." In the following year a man was put in the stocks for a similar offence. It is asserted that a man was placed in the Aynhoe stocks in 1846 for using bad language. Card-sharpers and the like often suffered in the stocks. It appears from the *Shrewsbury Chronicle* of May 1st, 1829, that the punishment of the stocks was inflicted "at Shrewsbury on three Birmingham youths for imposing on 'the flats' of the town with the games of 'thimble and pea' and 'prick the garter.'"

A very late instance of a man being placed in the stocks for gambling was recorded in the *Leeds Mercury*, under date of April 14th, 1860. "A notorious character," it is stated, "named John Gambles, of Stanningley, having been convicted some months ago for Sunday gambling, and sentenced to sit in the stocks for six hours, left the locality, returned lately, and suffered his punishment by sitting in the stocks from two till eight o'clock on Tuesday last." Several writers on this old form of punishment regard the foregoing as the latest instance of a person being confined in the stocks; it is, however, not the case, for one Mark Tuck, of Newbury, Berkshire, in 1872, was placed in them. The following particulars are furnished in *Notes and Queries*, 4th series, vol. x., p. 6:—"A novel scene was presented in the Butter and Poultry Market, at Newbury, on Tuesday (June 11th, 1872) afternoon. Mark Tuck, a rag and bone dealer, who for several years had been well known in the town as a man of intemperate habits, and upon whom imprisonment in Reading gaol had failed to produce any beneficial effect, was fixed in the stocks for drunkenness and disorderly conduct in the Parish Church on Monday evening. Twenty-six years had elapsed since the stocks were last used, and their reappearance created no little sensation and amusement, several hundreds of persons being attracted to the spot where they were fixed. Tuck was seated upon a stool, and his legs were secured in the stocks at a few minutes past one o'clock, and as the church clock, immediately facing him, chimed each quarter, he uttered expressions of thankfulness, and seemed anything but pleased at the laughter and derision of the crowd. Four hours having passed, Tuck was released, and by a little stratagem on the part of the police, he escaped without being interfered with by the crowd."

Attendance and repairing stocks formed quite important items in old parish accounts. A few entries drawn from the township account-books of Skipton, may be reproduced as examples :—

	s.	d.
April 16th, 1763.—For taking up a man and setting in ye stocks	2	0
March 27th, 1739.—For mending stocks—wood and iron work	9	6
July 12th, 1756.—For pillory and stocks renewing...	3	6
March 25th, 1776.—Paid John Lambert for repairing the stocks...	5	6
March 25th, 1776.—Paid Christ. Brown for repairing the stocks	4	6

During their later years, the Skipton stocks were used almost solely on Sundays. A practice prevailed at Skipton similar to the one we have described at Beverley. "At a certain stage in the morning service at the church," writes Mr. Dawson, the local historian, "the churchwardens of the town and country parishes withdrew, and headed by the old beadle walked through the streets of the town. If a person was found drunk in the streets, or even drinking in one of the inns,

From a Photo by] [*A. Whitford Anderson, Esq., Watford.*

STOCKS AND WHIPPING-POST, ALDBURY.

he was promptly escorted to the stocks, and impounded for the remainder of the morning. An imposing personage was the beadle. He wore a cocked hat, trimmed, as was his official coat, with gold, and he carried about with him in majestic style a trident staff. 'A terror to evildoers' he certainly was—at any rate, to those of tender years."* The churchwardens not infrequently partook of a slight refreshment during their Sunday morning rounds, and we remember seeing in the police reports of a Yorkshire town that some highly respectable representatives of the Church had been fined for drinking at an inn during their tour of inspection.

"At Bramhall, Cheshire," says Mr. Alfred Burton, to whom we are indebted for several illustrations and many valuable notes in this book, "the stocks were perfect till 1887, when the legstones were unfortunately taken away, and cannot now be found. Thomas Leah, about 1849, was the last person put into them. He went to the constable and asked to be placed in the stocks, a request that was granted, and he remained there all night. On the 9th August, 1822, two women were incarcerated in the stocks in the market

* W. H. Dawson's "History of Skipton." 1882.

place at Stockport, for three hours, one for getting drunk, the other for gross and deliberate scandal."

We give an illustration from a recent photograph by Mr. A. Whitford Anderson, of Watford, of the stocks and whipping-post at Aldbury, Hertfordshire. It presents one of the best pictures of these old time relics which has come under our notice. We have no desire for the

stocks and lash to be revived, but we hope these obsolete engines of punishments will long remain linking the past with the present.

In closing this chapter we must not omit to state that in the olden time persons refusing to assist in getting in the corn or hay harvest were liable to be imprisoned in the stocks. At the Northamptonshire Quarter Sessions held in 1688, the time was fixed at two days and one night.

The Drunkard's Cloak.

SEVERAL historians, dealing with the social life of England in bygone times, have described the wearing of a barrel after the manner of a cloak as a general mode of punishing drunkards, in force during the Commonwealth. There appears to be little foundation for the statement, and, after careful consideration, we have come to the conclusion that this mode of punishment was, as regards this country, confined to Newcastle-on-Tyne.

In the year 1655 was printed in London a work entitled, "England's Grievance Discovered in Relation to the Coal Trade," by Ralph Gardner, of Chirton, in the county of Northumberland, Gent. The book is dedicated to "Oliver, Lord Protector." Gardner not only gave a list of grievances, but suggested measures to reform them. It will be gathered from the following proposed remedy that he was not any advocate of half measures in punishing persons guilty of offences. He suggested that a law be created for death to those who should commit perjury, forgery, or bribery.

More than one writer has said that Gardner was executed in 1661, at York, for coining, but there is not any truth in the statement. We have proof that he was conducting his business after the year in which it is stated that he suffered death at the hands of the public executioner.

Gardner, in his work, gave depositions of witnesses to support his charges against "the tyrannical oppression of the magistrates of Newcastle-on-Tyne." "John Willis, of Ipswich," he writes, "upon his oath said, that he, and this deponent, was in Newcastle six months ago, and there he saw one Ann Bridlestone drove through the streets by an officer of the same corporation, holding a rope in his hand, the other end fastened to an engine called the branks, which is like a crown, it being of iron, which was musled over the head and face, with a great gag or tongue of iron forced into her mouth, which forced the blood out; and that is the punishment which the magistrates do inflict upon chiding and scoulding women; and he hath often seen the like done to others."

"He, this deponent, further affirms, that he

hath seen men drove up and down the streets, with a great tub or barrel opened in the sides, with a hole in one end to put through their heads, and so cover their shoulders and bodies, down to the small of their legs, and then close the same, called the new-fashioned cloak, and so make them march to the view of all beholders; and

BRANK AND DRUNKARD'S CLOAK, NEWCASTLE-ON-TYNE.

this is their punishment for drunkards and the like."

Several other forms of punishment are mentioned by Gardner. Drunkards, we gather, for the first offence were fined five shillings, to be given to the poor, or in default of payment within a week, were set in the stocks for six hours. For the second offence they had to be bound for good behaviour. Scolds had to be ducked over head and ears in a ducking-stool.

"I was certainly informed," wrote Gardner, "by persons of worth, that the punishments above are but gentle admonitions to what they knew was acted by two magistrates of Newcastle: one for killing a poor workman of his own, and being questioned for it, and condemned, compounded with King James for it, paying to a Scotch lord his weight in gold and silver, every seven years or thereabouts, etc. The other magistrate found a poor man cutting a few horse sticks in his wood, for which offence he bound him to a tree, and whipt him to death."

The Rev. John Brand, in 1789, published his "History of Newcastle-on-Tyne," and reproduced in it Gardner's notice of the drunkard's cloak. Brand gives a picture of the cloak, and Mr. J. R. Boyle, F.S.A., a leading authority on North Country bibliography, tells us that he believes it to be the first pictorial representation of the cloak. Our illustration is from Richardson's "Local Historian's Table Book." Mr. Walter Scott, publisher, of Newcastle-on-Tyne, has kindly lent us the block.

Dr. T. N. Brushfield, to whom we are under an

obligation for several of the facts included in this chapter, read before the British Archæological Association, February 15th, 1888, a paper on this theme. "It is rather remarkable," said Dr. Brushfield, "that no allusion to this punishment is to be found in the Newcastle Corporation accounts or other local documents." We have reproduced from Gardner's volume the only testimony we possess of the administration of the punishment in England. There are many traces of this kind of cloak on the continent. It is noticed in "Travels in Holland," by Sir William Brereton, under date of May 29th, 1634, as seen at Delft. John Evelyn visited Delft, on August 17th, 1641, and writes that in the Senate House "hangs a weighty vessel of wood, not unlike a butter-churn, which the adventurous woman that hath two husbands at one time is to wear on her shoulders, her head peeping out at the top only, and so led about the town, as a penance for her incontinence." Samuel Pepys has an entry in his diary respecting seeing a similar barrel at the Hague, in the year 1660. We have traces of this mode of punishment in Germany. John Howard, in his work entitled "The State of Prisons in England and Wales," 1784, thus writes: "Denmark.—Some (criminals) of the lower sort, as watchmen, coachmen, etc., are punished by being led through the city in what is called 'The Spanish Mantle.' This is a kind of heavy vest, something like a tub, with an aperture for the head, and irons to enclose the neck. I measured one at Berlin, 1ft. 8in. in diameter at the top, 2ft. 11in. at the bottom, and 2ft. 11in. high. . . . This mode of punishment is particularly dreaded, and is one cause that night robberies are never heard of in Copenhagen."

We may safely conclude that the drunkard's cloak was introduced into Newcastle from the Continent. The author of a paper published in 1862, under the title of "A Look at the Federal Army," after speaking of crossing the Susquehanna, has some remarks about punishments. "I was," says the writer, "extremely amused to see a 'rare' specimen of Yankee invention, in the shape of an original method of punishment drill. One wretched delinquent was gratuitously framed in oak, his head being thrust through a hole cut in one end of a barrel, the other end of which had been removed; and the poor fellow 'loafed' about in the most disconsolate manner, looking for all the world like a half-hatched chicken.

Another defaulter had heavy weights fastened to his wrists, his hands and feet being chained together." In conclusion, we are told that the punishments were as various as the crimes, but the man in the pillory-like barrel was deemed the most ludicrous.

PUNISHMENT OF A DRUNKARD.

The early English settlers in America introduced many English customs into the country. The pillory, stocks, ducking-stool, etc., were frequently employed. Drunkards were punished in various ways; sometimes they had to wear a large "D" in red, which was painted on a board or card, and suspended by a string round the neck.

At Haddon, Derbyshire, is a curious relic of bygone times, consisting of an iron handcuff or ring, fastened to some woodwork in the banqueting hall. If a person refused to drink the liquor assigned to him, or committed an offence against the convivial customs at the festive gatherings for which this ancient mansion was so famous, his wrist was locked in an upright position in the iron ring, and the liquor he had declined, or a quantity of cold water, was poured down the sleeve of his doublet.

Whipping and Whipping-Posts.

THE Anglo-Saxons whipped prisoners with a whip of three cords, knotted at the end. It was not an uncommon practice for mistresses to whip, or have their servants whipped, to death. William of Malmesbury relates a story to the effect that when King Ethelred was a child, he on one occasion displeased his mother, and she, not having a whip at hand, flogged him with some candles until he was nearly insensible with pain. "On this account," so runs the story, "he dreaded candles during the rest of his life to such a degree that he would never suffer the light of them to be introduced in his presence." During the Saxon epoch, flogging was generally adopted as means of punishing persons guilty of offences, whether slight or serious.

For a long time in our history, payments for using the lash formed important items in the municipal accounts of towns or parish accounts of villages.

Before the monasteries were dissolved, the poor

were relieved at them. No sooner had they passed away than the vagrants became a nuisance, and steps were taken to put a stop to begging; indeed, prior to this period attempts had been made to check wandering vagrants. They were referred to in the "Statute of Labourers," passed in the year 1349. Not a few enactments were made to keep down vagrancy. In the reign of Edward VI., in 1547, an Act was passed, from which it appears "that any person who had offered them work which they refused, was authorised to brand them on the breast with a V, hold them in slavery for two years, feed them during that period on bread and water, and hire them out to others." The Act failed on account of its severity, and was repealed in 1549.

It was in the reign of Henry VIII., and in the year 1530, that the famous Whipping Act was instituted, directing that vagrants were to be carried to some market town or other place, "and there tied to the end of a cart naked, and beaten with whips throughout such market town, or other place, till the body shall be bloody by reason of such whipping." Vagrants, after being whipped, had to take an oath that they would return to their native places, or where they had last dwelt for three years. Various temporary modifications were made in this Act, but it remained in force until the thirty-ninth year of the reign of Queen Elizabeth, when some important alterations were made. Persons were not to be publicly whipped naked, as previously, but from the middle upwards, and whipped until the body should be bloody. It was at this time that the whipping-post was substituted for the cart. Whipping-posts soon became plentiful. John Taylor, "the water poet," in one of his works, published in 1630, adverts to them as follows:

> "In London, and within a mile, I ween,
> There are jails or prisons full eighteen,
> And sixty whipping-posts and stocks and cages."

We give an illustration of the Waltham Abbey Whipping-Post and Stocks, as they appeared when they stood within the old wooden market-house, which was pulled down in 1853. The post bears on it the date 1598, and is 5 feet 9 inches high; it is strongly made of oak, with iron clasps for the hands when employed as a whipping-post, and for the feet when used as the stocks. It is rather more elaborate than others which have come under our notice. It will be observed the seat for the culprits placed in the stocks was beside one of the immense oak pillars of the market-house. They are now placed with the remains of the Pillory at the entrance of the schoolroom, on the south-west side of the church.

Some of the authorities regarded with greater favour the punishment at the whipping-post than at the cart tail. An old writer deals at some length with the benefit of the former. Says he: "If to put in execution the laws of the land be of any service to the nation, which few, I think, will deny, the benefits of the whipping-post must be very apparent, as being a necessary instrument to such an execution. Indeed, the service it does to a country is inconceivable. I, myself, know a man who had proceeded to lay his hand upon a silver spoon with a design to make it his own, but on looking round, and seeing the whipping-post in his way, he desisted from the theft. Whether he suspected that the post would impeach him or not, I will not pretend to determine; some folks were of opinion that he was afraid of *habeas corpus*. It is likewise an infallible remedy for all lewd and disorderly behaviour, which the chairman at sessions generally employs to restrain; nor is it less beneficial to the honest part of mankind

WALTHAM ABBEY WHIPPING-POST AND STOCKS.

than the dishonest, for though it lies immediately in the high road to the gallows, it has stopped many an adventurous young man in his progress thither." The records of the Worcester Corporation contain many references to old-time punishments. In the year 1656 was made in the bye-law book a note of the fact that for some years past a want has been felt "for certain instruments for applying to the execution of justice upon offenders, namely, the pillory, whipping-post, and gum-stoole." The Chamberlain was directed to obtain the same. We gather from the proceedings of the Doncaster Town Council that on the 5th of May, 1713, an order was made for the erection of a whipping-post, to be set up at the Stocks, Butcher-Cross, for punishing vagrants and sturdy beggars.

Notices of whipping sometimes appear in old church books. At Kingston-on-Thames, under date of September 8th, 1572, it is recorded in the parish register as follows: "This day in this towne was kept the sessions of Gayle Delyverye, and ther was hanged vj. persons, and xvj. taken for roges and vagabonds, and whypped aboyt the market-place, and brent in the ears."

At the Quarter Sessions in Devonshire, held at

Easter, 1598, it was ordered that the mothers of illegitimate children be whipped. The reputed fathers had to undergo a like punishment. A very strange order was made in the same county during the Commonwealth, and it was to the effect that every woman who had been the mother of an illegitimate child, and had not been previously punished, be committed for trial. Mr. Hamilton, in his work on the "Quarter Sessions from Queen Elizabeth to Queen Anne," has many curious notes on the subject. The Scotch pedlars and others who wended their way to push their trade in the West of England, ran a great risk of being whipped. At the Midsummer Sessions, in the year 1684, information was given to the court showing that certain Scotch pedlars, or other petty chapmen, were in the habit of selling their goods to the "greate damage and hindrance of shopp keepers." The Court passed measures for the protection of the local tradesmen, and directed the petty constables to apprehend the strangers, and without further ceremony to strip them naked, and whip them, or cause them to be openly flogged, and sent away.

The churchwardens' accounts of Barnsley contain references to the practice of whipping.

Charges as follow occur :

1622. William Roggers, for going with six wanderers to Ardsley ... ... ijd.
Mr. Garnett, for makinge them a pass ... ... iijd.
Richard White, for whippeinge them accordinge to law ... ... ijd.

The constable's accounts of the same town, from 1632 to 1636, include items similar to the following :

To Edward Wood, for whiping of three wanderers sent to their dwelling-place by Sir George Plint and Mr. Rockley ... ... iiijd.

It appears from the Corporation accounts of Congleton, Cheshire, that persons were whipped at the cart tail. We find it stated :

1637. paid to boy for whippinge John ffoxe 0 2 0
paid for a carte to tye the said ffoxe unto when he was whipped ... 0 2 0

The notorious Judge Jeffreys, on one occasion, in sentencing a woman to be whipped, said : "Hangman, I charge you to pay particular attention to this lady. Scourge her soundly, man ; scourge her till her blood runs down! It is Christmas, a cold time for madam to strip. See that you warm her shoulders thoroughly!"

At Worcester, in 1697, a new whipping-post was erected in the Corn Market, at a cost of 8s.

"Men and women," says a local historian, "were whipped here promiscuously in public till the close of the last century, if not later. Fourpence was the old charge for whipping male and female rogues."

The next note on whipping is drawn from the church register of Burnham, Bucks, and is one of several similar entries: "Benjamin Smat, and his wife and three children, vagrant beggars; he of middle stature, but one eye, was this 28th day of September, 1699, with his wife and children, openly whipped at Boveney, in the parish of Burnham, in the county of Bucks, according to ye laws. And they are assigned to pass forthwith from parish to parish by ye officers thereof the next direct way to the parish of St. [Se]pulchers, Lond., where they say they last inhabited three years. And they are limited to be at St. [Se]pulch within ten days next ensuing. Given under our hands and seals, Will. Glover, Vicar of Burnham, and John Hunt, Constable of Boveney." In some instances we gather from the entries in the parish registers, after punishing the vagrants in their own parish, the authorities recommended them to the tender mercy of other persons in whose hands they might fall.

At Durham, in the year 1690, a married woman named Eleanor Wilson, was publicly whipped in the market-place, between the hours of eleven and twelve o'clock, for being drunk on Sunday, April 20th.

Insane persons did not escape the lash. In the constable's accounts of Great Staughtan, Huntingdonshire, is an item:

1690-1.	Pd. in charges taking up a distracted woman, watching her, and whipping her next day	0	8	6

A still more remarkable charge is the following in the same accounts:

1710-1.	Pd. Thomas Hawkins for whipping 2 people yt had small-pox	0	0	8

In 1764, we gather from the *Public Ledger* that a woman, who is described as "an old offender," was conveyed in a cart from Clerkenwell Bridewell to Enfield, and publicly whipped at the cart's tail by the common hangman, for cutting down and destroying wood in Enfield Chase. She had to undergo the punishment three times.

Persons obtaining goods under false pretences were frequently flogged. In 1769, at Nottingham, a young woman, aged nineteen, was found guilty of this crime, and was, by order of the Court of Quarter Sessions, stripped to the waist and publicly whipped on market-day in the market-place. In the following year, a female found guilty of stealing a handkerchief from a draper's shop, was tied to the tail of a cart and whipped from Weekday-Cross to the Malt-Cross. It was at Nottingham, a few years prior to this time, that a soldier was severely punished for drinking the Pretender's health. The particulars are briefly told as follows in *Adams's Weekly Courant* for Wednesday, July 20th, to Wednesday, July 27th, 1737: "Friday last, a dragoon, belonging to Lord Cadogan's Regiment, at Nottingham, received 300 lashes, and was to receive 300 more at Derby, and to be drum'd out of the Regiment with halter about his neck, for drinking the Pretender's health."

Whipping at Wakefield appears to have been a common punishment. Payments like the following frequently occur in the constable's accounts:

1787, May 15,	Assistance at Whiping	3 men	...	0	3	0
July 6,	,, ,,	3 ,,	..	0	3	0
Aug. 17,	,, ,,	2 ,,	...	0	2	0
Sept. 7,	,, ,,	3 ,,	...	0	3	0

A fire occurred at Olney in 1783, and during

the confusion a man stole some ironwork. The crime was detected, and the man was tried and sentenced to be whipped at the cart's tail. Cowper, the poet, was an eye-witness to the carrying out of the sentence, and in a letter to the Rev. John Newton gives an amusing account of it. "The fellow," wrote Cowper, "seemed to show great fortitude; but it was all an imposition. The beadle who whipped him had his left hand filled with red ochre, through which, after every stroke, he drew the lash of the whip, leaving the appearance of a wound upon the skin, but in reality not hurting him at all. This being perceived by the constable, who followed the beadle to see that he did his duty, he (the constable) applied the cane, without any such management or precaution, to the shoulders of the beadle. The scene now became interesting and exciting. The beadle could by no means be induced to strike the thief hard, which provoked the constable to strike harder; and so the double flogging continued, until a lass of Silver End, pitying the pityful beadle, thus suffering under the hands of the pityless constable, joined the procession, and placing herself immediately behind the constable, seized him by his capillary club, and pulling him backward by the same, slapped his face with Amazonian fury. This concentration of events has taken up more of my paper than I intended, but I could not forbear to inform you how the beadle thrashed the thief, the constable the beadle, and the lady the constable, and how the thief was the only person who suffered nothing." It will be gathered from the foregoing letter that the severity of the whipping depended greatly on the caprice of the man who administered it.

A statute, in 1791, expressly forbade the whipping of female vagrants. This was certainly a much needed reform.

Mr. Samuel Carter Hall, born in the year 1800, in his interesting book entitled "Retrospect of a Long Life" (1883), relates that more than once he saw the cruel punishment inflicted.

On the 8th of May, 1822, a man was whipped through the streets of Glasgow by the hangman for taking part in a riot. He was the last person to undergo public whipping at the cart's tail in Glasgow.

At Coleshill are standing a whipping-post, pillory and stocks, and as might be expected they attract a good deal of attention from the visitors to this quiet Midland town. Several writers have stated that this is the only whipping-post remaining in this country; this is, however, a mistake, as we have shown in the present chapter. We have not been able to discover when last used. Our illustration is from a carefully executed drawing made some years ago.

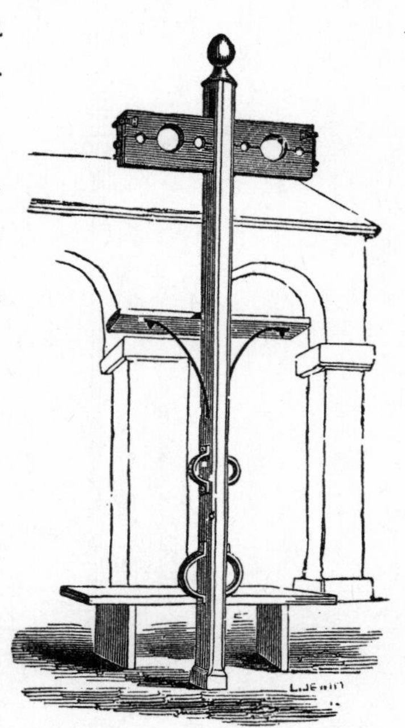

COLESHILL PILLORY, WHIPPING-POST, AND STOCKS.

The old town of Kirton-in-Lindsey, Lincolnshire, in bygone times was a place of importance, and amongst the names of those who have held its manor is that of Piers Gaveston, the favourite of Edward II. Near the modern police station is a post on which are irons, enabling it to be used as a whipping-post and stocks. No references relating to it can be found in the local old-time accounts or other documents. Old folk say that in years agone people were detained at the post by means of the irons, but no instances are remembered of a whip being employed.

It was formerly the custom in London and other places, at the time of executions, for parents to whip their children, so as to impress upon their minds the awful lessons of the gallows. Executions were very often occurring, for people were hanged for trifling offences. Down to the year 1808, the crime of stealing from the person above the value of a shilling was punishable with death. Children must have had a hard time of it, and been frequently flogged.

WHIPPING-POST, KIRTON-IN-LINDSEY.

Whipping servants was a common practice in the olden time. Pepys and other old writers make note of it.

The well-known "Diary of a Lady of Quality" contains some interesting glimpses of old days and ways. Under date of January 30th, 1760, Lady Francis Pennoyer, of Bullingham Court, Herefordshire, refers to one of her maids speaking in the housekeeper's room about a matter that was not to the credit of the family. My lady felt that there was truth in what the girl said, but it was not in her place to speak, and her ladyship resolved to make her know and keep her place. "She hath a pretty face," says the diarist, "and should not be too ready to speak ill of those above her in station. I should be very sorry to turn her adrift upon the world, and she hath but a poor home. Sent for her to my room, and gave her choice, either to be well whipped, or to leave the house instantly. She chose wisely, I think, and, with many tears, said I might do what I liked. I bade her attend my chamber to-morrow at twelve." Next day her ladyship writes in her diary: "Dearlove, my maid, came to my room, as I bade her. I bade her fetch the rod from what was my mother-in law's rod-closet, and kneel and ask pardon, which she did with tears. I made her prepare, and I whipped her well. The girl's flesh is plump and firm, and she is a cleanly person—such a one, not excepting my own daughters, who are thin, and one of them, Charlotte, rather sallow, as I have not whipped for a long time. She hath never been whipped before, she says, since she was a child (what can her mother and late lady have been about, I wonder?), and she cried out a great deal." Children and servants appear to have been frequently flogged at Bullingham Court, both by its lord and lady. In other homes similar practices prevailed.

"The Tutors Assistant"

(By George Cruikshank).

Public Penance.

CHURCH discipline in the olden days caused the highest and lowest in the land to perform penance in public. A notable instance of a king subjecting himself to this humiliating form of punishment is that of Henry II. The story of the King's quarrels with Becket, and of his unfortunate expression which led four knights to enact a tragic deed in Canterbury Cathedral, is familiar to the reader of history. After the foul murder of Becket had been committed, the King was in great distress, and resolved to do penance at the grave of the murdered Archbishop. Mounted on his horse, he rode to Canterbury, and on coming in sight of the Cathedral, he dismounted, and walked barefooted to Becket's shrine. He spent the day in prayer and fasting, and at night watched the relics of the saint. He next, in presence of the monks, disrobed himself, and presented his bare shoulders for them to lash.

At Canossa, in the winter of 1077, was performed a most degrading act of penance by

Emperor Henry IV. of Germany. He had been excommunicated by Pope Gregory VII., and had suffered much on that account. He resolved to see the Pope, and, if possible, obtain absolution. The Emperor made a long and toilsome journey in the cold, in company with his loving wife Bertha, his infant son, and only one knight. The Pope refused to see the Emperor until he had humbled himself at the gates of the castle. "On a dreary winter morning," say Baring-Gould and Gilman, in their "History of Germany," "with the ground deep in snow, the King, the heir of a line of emperors, was forced to lay aside every mark of royalty, was clad in the thin white dress of the penitent, and there fasting, he awaited the pleasure of the Pope in the castle yard. But the gates did not unclose. A second day he stood, cold, hungry, and mocked by vain hope." On the close of the third day, we are told that he was received and pardoned by the Pope.

The romantic story of Eleanor Cobham, first mistress and afterwards wife of Humphrey, Duke of Gloucester, is one of considerable interest in illustrating the strange beliefs of the olden times. The Duchess was tried in the year 1441, for treason and witchcraft. It transpired that two of her accomplices had made, by her direction, a waxen image of the reigning monarch, Henry VI. They had placed it before a slow fire, believing that the King's life would waste away as the figure did. In the event of Henry's death, the Duke of Gloucester, as the nearest heir to the house of Lancaster, would have been crowned king. On the 9th November, sentence was pronounced upon the Duchess: it was to the effect that she perform public penance in three open places in London, and end her days in prison in the Isle of Man. The manner of her doing penance was as follows: "On Monday, the 13th, she came by water from Westminster, and landing at Temple Bridge, walked at noon-day through Fleet Street, bearing a waxen taper of two pounds weight, to St. Paul's, where she offered it at the high altar. On the Wednesday following, she landed at the Old Swan, and passed through Bride Street, Gracechurch Street, and to Leadenhall, and at Cree Church, near Aldgate, made her second offering. On the ensuing Friday she was put on shore at Queenhithe, whence she proceeded to St. Michael's Church, Cornhill, and so completed her penance. In each of these processions her head was covered only by a kerchief; her feet were bare; scrolls, containing a narrative of her crime, were affixed to her white dress; and she was received and attended by the Mayor, Sheriff, and Companies of London."

The historian, biographer, poet, playwright, and story-teller have all related details of the career of Jane Shore. A sad tale it is, but one which has always been popular both with gentle and simple. It is not necessary to relate here at length the story of her life. She was born in London, was a woman of considerable personal charms, and could do what few ladies of her time were able to accomplish—namely, read well and write. When some sixteen or seventeen years of age, she married William Shore, a goldsmith and banker, of Lombard Street. She lived with her husband seven years, but about 1470, left him to become one of the mistresses of Edward IV. Her beauty, wit, and pleasant behaviour rendered her popular at Court. The King died in 1483, and within two months she was charged by Richard III. with sorcery and witchcraft, but the charges could not be sustained. Her property, equal to about £20,000 at the present time, was taken from her by the King. He afterwards caused her to be brought before the Ecclesiastical Court and tried for incontinence, and for the crime she had to do penance in the streets of London. Perhaps we cannot do better than quote Rowe's drama to relate this part of her story:

> Submissive, sad, and lonely was her look;
> A burning taper in her hand she bore;
> And on her shoulders, carelessly confused,
> With loose neglect her lovely tresses hung;
> Upon her cheek a faintish flush was spread;
> Feeble she seemed, and sorely smit with pain;
> While, barefoot as she trod the flinty pavement,
> Her footsteps all along were marked with blood.
> Yet silent still she passed, and unrepining;
> Her streaming eyes bent ever on the earth,
> Except when, in some bitter pang of sorrow,
> To heaven, she seemed, in fervent zeal to raise,
> And beg that mercy man denied her here.

We need not go into details respecting her life from this time, but briefly state that it is a popular error to suppose that she was starved in a ditch, and that the circumstance gave rise to the name of a part of London known as Shoreditch. The black-letter ballad in the Pepys collection, which makes Jane Shore die of hunger after doing penance, and a man suffer death on the gallows for giving her bread, is without foundation. She died about 1533 or 1534, when she was upwards of eighty years of age. It is asserted that she strewed flowers at the funeral of Henry VII.

A curious act of penance was performed in Hull, in the year 1534, by the Vicar of North Cave. He appears to have made a study of the works of the Reformers who had settled in Antwerp, and sent over their books to England. In a sermon preached in the Holy Trinity Church, Hull, he advocated their teaching, and for this he was tried for heresy and convicted. He recanted, and, as an act of penance, one Sunday walked round the church barefooted, with only his shirt on, and carrying a large faggot in his hand to represent the punishment he deserved. On the next market-day, in a similar manner, he walked round the market-place of the town.

In the year 1602, a man named Cuthbert Pearson Foster, residing in the parish of St. Nicholas, Durham, was brought before the Ecclesiastical Court, charged with "playing at nine-holes upon the Sabbath day in time of divine service," and was condemned to stand once in the parish church during service, clad in a white sheet. In the following year, the four church-wardens—Rowland Swinburn, William Harp, Richard Surtees, and Cuthbert Dixon, men esteemed in Durham, and holding good positions

—were found guilty and admonished for a serious breach of duty, "for not searching who was absent from the church on the Sabbath and festive days, for it is credibly reported that drinking, banqueting, and playing at cards, and other lawless games, are used in their parish in alehouses, and they never made search thereof."

Of persons in the humble ranks of life who have performed public penance in white sheets in churches, for unchastity, there are numerous entries in parish registers. For immorality, prior to marriage, man and wife were sometimes obliged to do penance. The Rev. Dr. J. Charles Cox found particulars of a case of this kind recorded in the Wooley MSS., in the British Museum, where a married couple, in the reign of James I., performed penance in Wirksworth Church.

In parish registers are records like the following, drawn from the Roxby (Lincolnshire) parish register: "Memorandum.—Michael Kirby and Dixon, Wid. had 2 Bastard Children, one in 1725, ye other in 1727, for which they did publick pennance in our P'ish Church." "Michael Kirby and Anne Dixon, both together did publick penance in our Parish Churche, Feb. ye 25th, 1727, for adultery."

A memorandum in the parish register of North Aston, Oxfordshire, states: "That Mr. Cooper sent in a form of penance by Mr. Wakefield, of Deddington, that Catherine King should do penance in ye parish church of North Aston, ye sixth day of March, 1740, and accordingly she did. Witness, Will Vaughan, Charles May, John Baillis, Churchwardens." We learn from the same records that another person, who had become a mother before she was made a wife, left the parish to avoid doing public penance.

In the old churchwardens' accounts of Wakefield, are several items bearing on this subject, and amongst the number are the following:

	£	s.	d.
1679.—To Jos. Green for black bess penanc sheet...	00	05	06
1709.—Allowed the Parish Churchwardens for goeing to Leeds with ye man and woman to doe penance	0	5	0
1725.—June 13. Paid Jno. Briggs for the Lent of 3 sheets for 3 persons to do pennance ...	00	01	6
1731.—Nov. 6. Paid for the loan of two white Sheets			6
1732.—Oct. 8. Pd. for the loan of 7 sheets for penances		1	9
1735.—Nov. 1. Pd. for a sheet that —— had to do penance in		1	0

	s.	d.
1736.—Sep. 27. Pd. for two sheets ye women did penans in		8
1736.—Oct. 10. Pd. for a sheet for Stringer to do penance in		4
1737.—June 23. Pd. for a sheet for Eliza Redhead penance		4
1750.—Dec. 26. To Priestly for a sheet & attending a woman's penance	5	0

"On February 27th, 1815," says Mr. John W. Walker, "William Hepworth, a shoemaker, did penance in the Parish Church for defaming the character of an old woman named Elizabeth Blacketer. They both lived in Cock and Swan Yard, Westgate, and the suit was carried on by one George Robinson, an attorney, out of spite to the cobbler."

"On Sunday, August 25th, 1850, a penance was performed in the Parish Church, by sentence of the Ecclesiastical Court, on a person who had defamed the character of a lady in Wakefield. A recantation was repeated by the penitent after the Vicar, and then signed by the interested parties."*

The historian of Cleveland, Mr. George Markham Tweddell, furnishes us with a copy of a document enjoining penance to be performed in 1766, by James Beadnell, of Stokesley, in the

* Walker's "History of Wakefield Cathedral."

diocese of York, tailor: "The said James Beadnell shall be present in the Parish Church of Stokesley, aforesaid, upon Sunday, being the fifth, twelfth, and nineteenth day of January instant, in the time of Divine service, between the hours of ten and eleven in the forenoon of the same day, in the presence of the whole congregation then assembled, being barehead, barefoot, and barelegged, having a white sheet wrapped about him from the shoulder to the feet, and a white wand in his hand, where, immediately after the reading of the Gospel, he shall stand upon some form or seat, before the pulpit or place where the minister readeth prayers, and say after him as forthwith: 'Whereas, I, good people, forgetting my duty to Almighty God, have committed the detestable sin of adultery with Ann Andrewes, and thereby have provoked the heavy wrath of God against me to the great danger of my soul and evil example of others. I do earnestly repent, and am heartily sorry for the same, desiring Almighty God, for the merits of Jesus Christ, to forgive me both this and all other my offences, and also ever hereafter so to assist me with His Holy Spirit, that I never fall into the like offence again; and for that end and purpose, I desire you all here present to pray for me, saying, 'Our Father, which art in heaven,' and so forth."

Towards the close of the last century, it was the practice of women doing penance at Poulton Church, Lancashire, to pass along the aisles barefooted, clothed in a white sheet, and having in each hand a lighted candle. The last time the ceremony was performed, we are told, the cries of the poor girl melted the heart of the people, and the well-disposed raised a clamour against it, and caused the practice to be discontinued.

The Rev. Thomas Jackson, the popular Wesleyan minister, was born at Sancton, a village on the Yorkshire Wolds, in 1783. Writing of his earlier years spent in his native village, he describes two cases of public penance which he witnessed. "A farmer's son," says Mr. Jackson, "the father of an illegitimate child, came into church at the time of divine service, on the Lord's day, covered with a sheet, having a white wand in his hand; he walked barefoot up the aisle, stood over against the desk where the prayers were read, and then repeated a confession at the dictation of the clergyman; after which he walked out of the church. The other case was that of a young woman,

'Who bore unhusbanded a mother's name.'

She also came into the church barefoot, covered with a sheet, bearing a white wand, and went through the same ceremony. She had one advantage which the young man had not. Her long hair so completely covered her face that not a feature could be seen. In a large town, few persons would have known who she was, but in a small village every one is known, and no public delinquent can escape observation, and the censure of busy tongues. These appear to have been the last cases of the kind that occurred at Sancton. The sin was perpetuated, but the penalty ceased; my father observed that the rich offenders evaded the law, and then the authorities could not for shame continue to inflict its penalty upon the labouring classes."*

In the month of April, 1849, penance was performed at Ditton Church, Cambridgeshire.

The Church of East Clevedon, Somersetshire, on July 30th, 1882, was the scene of a man performing penance in public, and the act attracted much attention in the newspapers of the time.

*Rev. Thomas Jackson's "Recollections of my own Life and Times." 1873.

The Repentance-Stool.

THE records of church-life in Scotland, in bygone times, contain many allusions to the repentance-stool. A very good specimen of this old-time relic may be seen in the Museum of the Society of Antiquaries, at Edinburgh. It is from the church of Old Greyfriars, of Edinburgh. In the same museum is a sackcloth, or gown of repentance, formerly used at the parish church of West Calder.

Persons guilty of adultery were frequently placed on the repentance-stool, and rebuked before the congregation assembled for public worship. The ordeal was a most trying one. Severe laws have been passed in Scotland to check adultery. "In the First Book of Discipline," says the Rev. Charles Rogers, LL.D., "the Reformers demanded that adulterers should be put to death. Their desire was not fully complied with, but in 1563 Parliament enacted that 'notour adulterers'—meaning those of whose illicit connection a child had been born—should be executed." Dr. Rogers and other authorities assert that the penalty was occasionally inflicted.

Paul Methven, minister at Jedburgh, in the year 1563, admitted that he had been guilty of adultery. The General Assembly conferred with the Lords of the Council respecting his conduct.

REPENTANCE STOOL, FROM OLD GREYFRIARS, EDINBURGH.

Three years later, we are told, that he was "permitted to prostrate himself on the floor of the Assembly, and with weeping and howling to entreat for pardon." His sentence was as follows: "That in Edinburgh, as the capital, in Dundee, as his native town, and in Jedburgh, the scene of his ministrations, he should stand in sackcloth at the church door, also on the repentance-stool, and for two Sundays in each place."

A man, on his own confession, was tried for adultery at the Presbytery of Paisley, on November 16th, 1626, and directed to "stand and abyde six Sabbaths barefooted and barelegged at the kirk-door of Paisley between the second and third bell-ringing, and thereafter to goe to the place of public repentance during the said space of six Sabbaths."

At Stow, in 1627, for a similar crime, a man was condemned to "sittin' eighteen dyetts" upon the stool of repentance. Particulars of many cases similar to the foregoing may be found in the pages of "Social Life in Scotland," by the Rev. Charles Rogers, in "Old Church Life in Scotland," by the Rev. Andrew Edgar, and in other works.

Notes bearing on this subject sometimes find their way into the newspapers, and a couple of paragraphs from the *Liverpool Mercury* may be quoted. On November 18th, 1876, it was stated that "in a church in the Black Isle, Ross-shire, on a recent Sunday, a woman who had been guilty of transgressing the seventh commandment was condemned to the 'cutty-stool,' and sat during the whole service with a black shawl thrown over her head." A note in the issue for 22nd February, 1884, says that "one of the ringleaders in the Sabbatarian riots at Strome Ferry, in June last, was recently publicly rebuked and admonished on the 'cutty-stool,' in the Free Church, Lochcarron, for an offence against the moral code, which, according to Free Church discipline in the Highlands, could not be expiated in any other way."

The Ducking-Stool.

SCOLDING women in the olden times were treated as offenders against the public peace, and for their transgressions were subjected to several cruel modes of punishment. The Corporations of towns during the Middle Ages made their own regulations for punishing persons guilty of crimes which were not rendered penal by the laws of the land. The punishments for correcting scolds differed greatly in various parts of the country. It is clear, from a careful study of the history of mediæval times, that virtue and amiability amongst the middle and lower classes, generally speaking, did not prevail. The free use of the tongue gave rise to riots and feuds to an extent which it is difficult for us to realise at the present day. A strong feeling against scolding women came down to a late period. Readers of Boswell's "Life of Johnson" will remember how the Doctor, in reply to a remark made by a celebrated Quaker lady, Mrs. Knowles, observed: "Madam, we have different modes of restraining evil—stocks for men, a ducking-stool for women, and a pound for beasts."

The cucking-stool in the early history of England must not be confounded with the ducking-stool. They were two distinct machines. It appears, from a record in the "Domesday Book," that as far back as the days of Edward the Confessor, any man or woman detected giving false measure in the city of Chester was fined four shillings; and for brewing bad ale, was placed in the *cathedra stercoris*. It was a degrading mode of chastisement, the culprits being seated in the chair at their own doors or in some public place. At Leicester, in 1467, the local authorities directed "scolds to be punished by the mayor on a cuck-stool before their own doors, and then carried to the four gates of the town." According to Borlase's "Natural History of Cornwall," in that part of the country the cucking-stool was used "as a seat of infamy, where strumpets and scolds, with bare feet and head, were condemned to abide the derision of those that passed by, for such time as the bailiffs of the manors, which had the privilege of such jurisdiction, did approve." Ale-wives in Scotland in bygone times who sold bad ale were placed in the cucking-stool. In the year 1555, we learn from Thomas Wright that "it was enacted by the queen-regent of Scotland that itinerant singing women should be put on the cuck-stoles of every burgh or town; and the first 'Homily against Contention,' part 3, published in 1562, sets forth that 'in all well-ordered cities common brawlers and scolders be punished with a notable kind of paine, as to be *set on* the cucking-stole, pillory, or such-like.' By the statute of 3 Henry VIII., carders and spinners of wool who were convicted of fraudulent practices were to be *sett upon* the pillory or the cukkyng-stole, man or woman, as the case shall require." We agree with Mr. Wright when he observes that the preceding passages are worded in such a manner as not to lead us to suppose that the offenders were ducked. In the course of time the terms cucking and ducking stools became synonymous, and implied the machines for the ducking of scolds in water.

In some places the term thewe was used for a cucking-stool. This was the case at Hedon, and it occurs in pleadings at Chester before the itinerant justices and Henry VII., when George Grey, Earl of Kent, claims the right in his manor of Bushton and Ayton of punishing brawlers by the thewe.* Other instances of its use might be cited.

An intelligent Frenchman, named Misson, visited England about 1700, and has left on record one of the best descriptions of a ducking-stool that has been written. It occurs in a work entitled "Travels in England." "The way of punishing scolding women," he writes, "is pleasant enough. They fasten an arm chair to the end of two beams, twelve or fifteen feet long, and parallel to each other, so that these two pieces of wood, with their two ends, embrace the chair, which hangs between them upon a sort of axle, by which means it plays freely, and always remains in the natural horizontal position in which the chair should be, that a person may sit conveniently in it, whether you raise it or let it down. They set up a post on the bank of a pond or river, and over this post they lay, almost in equilibrio, the two pieces of wood, at one end of which the chair hangs just over the water. They place the woman in this chair, and so plunge her into the water, as often as the sentence directs, in order to cool her immoderate heat." In some instances the ducking was carried to such an

* Boyle's "Hedon." 1895.

extent as to cause death. An old chap-book, without date, is entitled, "Strange and Wonderful Relation of the Old Woman who was Drowned at Ratcliff Highway a fortnight ago." It appears from this work that the poor woman was dipped too often, for at the conclusion of the operation she was found to be dead. We reproduce from this quaint chap-book a picture of the ducking-

DUCKING-STOOL FROM A CHAP-BOOK.

stool. It will be observed that it is not a stationary machine, but one which can be wheeled to and from the water. Similar ducking-stools were usually kept in some convenient building, and ready to be brought out for immediate use, but in many places the ducking-stools were permanent fixtures.

Old municipal accounts and records contain

many references to this subject. Cole, a Cambridge antiquary, collected numerous curious items connected with this theme. In some extracts made from the proceedings of the Vice-Chancellor's Court, in the reign of Elizabeth, it is stated: "Jane Johnson, adjudged to the ducking-stool for scolding, and commuted her penance." The next person does not appear to have been so fortunate as Jane Johnson, who avoided punishment by paying a fine of about five shillings. It is recorded: "Katherine Saunders, accused by the churchwardens of Saint Andrews for a common scold and slanderer of her neighbours, was adjudged to the ducking-stool."

We find in one of Cole's manuscript volumes, preserved in the British Museum, a graphic sketch of this ancient mode of punishment. He says: "In my time, when I was a boy, I lived with my grandmother in the great corner house at the foot, 'neath the Magdalen College, Cambridge, and rebuilt since by my uncle, Joseph Cook. I remember to have seen a woman ducked for scolding. The chair was hung by a pulley fastened to a beam about the middle of the bridge, in which [he means the chair, of course, not the bridge] the woman was confined, and let down three times, and then taken out. The bridge was then of timber, before the present stone bridge of one arch was built. The ducking-stool was constantly hanging in its place, and on the back of it were engraved devils laying hold of scolds, etc. Some time afterwards a new chair was erected in the place of the old one, having the same devices carved upon it, and well painted and ornamented. When the new bridge of stone was erected, in 1754, this chair was taken away, and I lately saw the carved and gilt back of it nailed up by the shop of one Mr. Jackson, a whitesmith, in the Butcher's Row, behind the Town Hall, who offered it to me, but I did not know what to do with it. In October, 1776, I saw in the old Town Hall a third ducking-stool, of plain oak, with an iron bar in front of it, to confine the person in the seat, but I made no inquiries about it. I mention these things as the practice of ducking scolds in the river seems now to be totally laid aside." Mr. Cole died in 1782, so did not long survive the writing of the foregoing curious notes.

The Sandwich ducking-stool was embellished with men and women scolding. On the cross-bar were carved the following words :

"Of members ye tonge is worst or best,—an
Yll tonge oft doeth breede unrest."

Boys, in his "Collections for the History of Sandwich," published in 1792, remarks that the ducking-stool was preserved in the second storey of the Town Hall, along with the arms, offensive and defensive, of the Trained Bands. Boys's book includes some important information on old-time punishments. In the year 1534, it is recorded that two women were banished from Sandwich for immorality. To deter them from coming back to the town, it was decided that "if they return, one of them is to suffer the pain of sitting over the coqueen-stool, and the other is to be set three days in the stocks, with an allowance of only bread and water, and afterwards to be placed in the coqueen-stool and dipped to the chin." A woman, in the year 1568, was "carted and banished." At Sandwich, Ipswich, and some other places, as a punishment

SANDWICH DUCKING-STOOL.

for scolding and other offences it was not an uncommon thing to compel the transgressors to carry a wooden mortar round the town.

Respecting the cost of erecting a ducking-stool, we find a curious and detailed account in the parish books of Southam, Warwickshire, for the year 1718. In the first place, a man was sent from Southam to Daventry to make a drawing of the ducking-stool of that town, at a cost of three shillings and twopence. The sum of one pound one shilling and eightpence is charged for labour and material in making and fixing the engine of punishment. An entry of ten shillings is made for painting it, which appears a rather heavy amount when we observe that the carpenter only charged a little over a pound for labour and timber. Perhaps, like the good folk of Sandwich, the authorities of Southam had their chair ornamented with artistic portraits and enriched with poetic quotations. The blacksmith had to furnish ironwork, etc., at a cost of four shillings and sixpence. For carrying the stool to its proper place half-a-crown was paid. Lastly, nine shillings and sixpence had to be expended to make the pond deeper, so that the ducking-stool might work in a satisfactory manner. The total amount reached £2 11s. 4d. At Coventry, in the same county, we find traces of two ducking-stools, and respecting them Mr. W. G. Fretton, F.S.A., supplies us with some curious details. The following notes are drawn from the Leet Book, under date of October 11th, 1597: "Whereas there are divers and sundrie disordered persons (women) within this citie that be scolds, brawlers, disturbers, and disquieters of theire neighbors, to the great offence of Almightie God and the breach of Her Majestie's peace: for the reformation of such abuses, it is ordered and enacted at this leet, that if any disordered and disquiet persons of this citie do from henceforth scold or brawle with their neighbo'rs or others, upon complaint thereof to the Alderman of the ward made, or to the Maior for the time being, they shall be committed to the cooke-stoole lately appointed for the punishment of such offenders, and thereupon be punished for their deserts, except they or everie of them, do presentlie paie iijs iijd for their redemption from that punishment to the use of the poore of this citie." The old accounts of the City of Coventry contain numerous items bearing on the ducking-stool.

In a volume of "Miscellaneous Poems," by

Benjamin West, of Weedon Beck, Northamptonshire, published in 1780, we find some lines entitled, "The Ducking-Stool," which run :

"There stands, my friend, in yonder pool,
An engine called the ducking-stool,
By legal pow'r commanded down,
The joy and terror of the town,
If jarring females kindle strife,
Give language foul or lug the coif;
If noisy dames should once begin
To drive the house with horrid din,
Away, you cry, you'll grace the stool,
We'll teach you how your tongue to rule.
The fair offender fills the seat,
In sullen pomp, profoundly great.
Down in the deep the stool descends,
But here, at first, we miss our ends ;
She mounts again, and rages more
Than ever vixen did before.
So, throwing water on the fire
Will make it but burn up the higher;
If so, my friend, pray let her take
A second turn into the lake,
And, rather than your patience lose,
Thrice and again repeat the dose.
No brawling wives, no furious wenches,
No fire so hot, but water quenches.
In Prior's skilful lines we see
For these another recipe :
A certain lady, we are told
(A lady, too, and yet a scold),
Was very much reliev'd, you'll say

By water, yet a different way;
A mouthful of the same she'd take,
Sure not to scold, if not to speak."

A footnote to the poem states: "To the honour of the fair sex in the neighbourhood of R——y, this machine has been taken down (as useless) several years." Most probably, says Mr. Jewitt, the foregoing refers to Rugby. In the old accounts of that town several items occur, as for example:

1721. June 5. Paid for a lock for ye ducking-stool, and spent in towne business ... ... 1s. 2d.
1739. Sept. 25. Ducking-stool repaired. And Dec. 21, 1741. A chain for ducking-stool ... 2s. 4d

Mr. Petty, F.S.A., in a note to Mr. Jewitt, which is inserted in *The Reliquary* for January, 1861, states that the Rugby ducking-stool "was placed on the west side of the horsepool, near the foot-path leading from the Clifton Road towards the new churchyard. Part of the posts to which it was affixed were visible until very lately, and the National School is now erected on its site. The last person who underwent the punishment was a man for beating his wife about forty years since; but although the ducking-stool has been long removed, the ceremony of immersion in the horse-pond was recently inflicted on an inhabitant for brutality towards his wife." The Rugby ducking-stool was of the trebuchet form, somewhat similar to one which was in use at Broadwater, near Worthing, and which has been frequently engraved. We reproduce an illustration of the latter from the *Wiltshire Archæological Magazine*, which represents it as it appeared in the year 1776. It was in existence at a much later period.

DUCKING-STOOL, BROADWATER, NEAR WORTHING.

Its construction was very simple, consisting of a short post let into the ground at the edge of a pond, bearing on the top a transverse beam, one end of which carried the stool, while the other end was secured by a rude chair. We are told, in an old description of this ducking-stool, that the beam could be moved horizontally, so as to bring the seat to the edge of the pond, and that when the beam was moved back, so as to place the seat and the person in it over the pond, the beam was worked up and down like a see-saw, and so the person in the seat was ducked. When the machine was not in use, the end of the beam which came on land was secured to a stump in the ground by a padlock, to prevent the village children from ducking each other.

Mr. T. Tindall Wildridge, author of several important local historical works, says that the great profligacy of Hull frequently gave rise in olden times to very stringent exercise of the magisterial authority. Not infrequently this was at the direct instigation and sometimes command of the Archbishop of York. Occasionally the cognisance of offences was retrospective. Thus, in November, 1620, it was resolved by the Bench of Magistrates, then composed of the Aldermen of the town, that such as had been "faltie for bastardes" should be carted about the town and afterwards "ducked in the water for their faults, for which they have hitherto escaped punishment." At a little later period, in England, in the days of the Commonwealth, it was enacted on May 14th, 1650, that adultery should be punished with death, but there is not any record of the law taking effect. The Act was repealed at the Restoration. About a century before this period, namely, in 1563, in the Scottish Parliament, this crime was made a capital offence. In New England, in the year 1662, several men and women suffered for this crime.

Resuming our notes on the Hull ducking-stool, we find, according to Hadley, the historian, that in the year 1731 Mr. Beilby, who held the office of town's husband, was ordered to take care that a ducking-stool should be provided at the South-end for the benefit of scolds and unquiet women. Six years later, John Hilbert published a view of the town of Hull, in which there is a representation of the ducking-stool. Mr. Wildridge has found traces of another local ducking-stool. He states that in some accounts belonging to the eighteenth century there is a charge for tarring a ducking-stool situated on the Haven-side, on the east side of the town.

At the neighbouring town of Beverley are traces of this old mode of punishment, and in the town records are several notes bearing on the subject. Brewers of bad beer and bakers of bad bread, as well as scolding women, were placed in the ducking-stool.

The Leeds ducking-stool was at Quarry Hill,

near the Spa. At the Court of Quarter Sessions, held in the town in July, 1694, it was "ordered that Anne, the wife of Phillip Saul, a person of lewd behaviour, be ducked for daily making strife and discord amongst her neighbours." A similar order was made against Jane Milner and Elizabeth Wooler.

We find in the Session records of Wakefield, for 1602, the following:

> "Punishm^{t} of Hall and Robinson, scolds: fforasmuch as Katherine Hall and M'garet Robinson, of Wakefield, are great disturbers and disquieters of their neighbours w'thin the toune of Wakefield, by reason of their daily scolding and chydering, the one w'th the other, for reformacon whereof ytt it is ordered that if they doe hereafter continue their former course of life in scolding and brawling, that then John Mawde, the high constable there, shall cause them to be soundlye ducked or cucked on the cuckstool at Wakefield for said misdemeanour."

In the records of Wakefield Sessions, under date of October 5th, 1671, the following appears:

> "Forasmuch as Jane, the wife of William Farrett of Selby, shoemaker, stands indicted at this sessions for a common scold, to the great annoyance and disturbance of her neighbours, and breach of His Majesty's peace. It is therefore ordered that the said Jane Farrett, for the said offence be openly ducked, and ducked three times over the head and ears by the constables of Selby aforesaid, for which this shall be their warrant."

At Bradford, the ducking-stool was formerly at the Beck, near to the Parish Church, and on the formation of the canal it was removed, but only a short distance from its original position. Still lingering in the West Riding of Yorkshire, we find in the parish accounts of East Ardsley, a village near to Wakefield, the following item :

1683-4. Paid John Crookes for repairing stool... 1s. 8d.

Norrisson Scatcherd, in his "History of Morley," and William Smith, in his "Morley Ancient and Modern," give interesting details of the ducking-stool at Morley.

Not far distant from Morley is Calverley, and in the Constable's accounts of the village it is stated :

1728. Paid Jeremy Booth for powl for ducking-stool 2s.

Mr. Joseph Wilkinson, the historian of Worsborough, near Barnsley, mentions two ducking-ponds in the township—one in the village of Worsborough, another near to the Birdwell toll-bar ; and, judging from the frequency with which ducking-stools were repaired by the township, it would seem they were often brought into requisition. The following extracts are drawn from the parish accounts :

1703.	For mending ye cuck-stool	£0	0	6
1721.	Ducking-stool mending	0	1	8
1725.	For mending and hanging ye cuck-stool...	0	1	0
1730.	Pd. Thos. Moorhouse for mending ye stocks and cuck-stool	0	1	0
"	Pd. Jno. South for 2 staples for ye cucking-stool	0	0	4
1731.	Thos. Moorhouse for mending ye ducking-stool	0	1	0
1734-5.	To ye ducking-stool mending	0	0	6
1736.	For mending ye ducking-stool	0	10	0
1737.	John Ellot, for ye ducking-stool and sheep-fold door	0	14	6

Mr. W. H. Dawson, the historian of Skipton, has devoted considerable attention to the old-time punishments of the town, and the first reference he was able to discover amongst the old accounts of the township is the following:

1734. October 2nd. To Wm. Bell, for ducking-stool making and wood ... ... 8s. 6d.

"This must," says Mr. Dawson, "surely mean that the chair was changed, for the amount is too small for the entire apparatus. In this case a ducking-stool must have existed before 1734, which is very likely." In the same Skipton township account-book is an entry as follows:

1743. October. Ben Smith for ducking-stool ... 4s. 6d.

Twenty-five years later we find a payment as follows:

1768. October 17th. Paid John Brown
for new ducking-stool ... £1 0s. 11½d.

Mr. Dawson has not been able to discover the exact date when the ducking-stool fell into disuse, but has good reason for believing that it was about 1770. We gather from a note sent to us by Mr. Dawson that: "A ducking-pond existed at Kirkby, although it had not been used within the memory of any living person. Scolds of both sexes were punished by being ducked; indeed, in the last observance of the custom, a tailor and his wife were ducked together, in view of a large gathering of people. The husband had applied for his wife to undergo the punishment on account of her quarrelsome nature, but the magistrate decided that one was not better than the other, and he ordered a joint punishment! Back to back, therefore, husband and wife were chaired and dipped into the cold water of the pond! Whether it was in remembrance of this old observance or not cannot be definitely said, but it is nevertheless a fact that in East Lancashire, in 1880, a man who had committed some violation of morals was forcibly taken by a mob, and dragged several times through a pond until he had expressed penitence for his act."

We have found several allusions to the Derby ducking-stool, Wooley, writing in 1772, states that "over against the steeple [All Saint's] is St. Mary's Gate, which leads down to the brook near the west side of St. Werburgh's Church, over which there is a bridge to Mr. Osborne's mill, over the pool of which stands the ducking-stool. A joiner named Thomas Timmins repaired it in 1729, and charged as follows:

To ye Cuckstool, the stoop	0	01	0
2 Foot and ½ of Ioyce for a Rayle... ...	0	00	5
Ja. Ford, junr., ½ day at Cuckstool ...	0	00	7

The Chesterfield ducking-stool was pulled down towards the close of the last century. It is stated that in the latter part of its existence it was chiefly used for punishing refractory paupers.

The Scarborough ducking-stool was formerly placed on the old pier, and was last used about the year 1795, when a Mrs. Gamble was ducked. The chair is preserved in the Museum of the Scarborough Philosophical Society. We are indebted to Dr. T. N. Brushfield for an excellent drawing of it.

An object which attracts much attention from visitors to the interesting museum at Ipswich is the ducking-stool of the town. We give a carefully executed drawing of it. It is described as a strong-backed arm-chair, with a wrought-iron rod, about an inch in diameter, fastened to each arm in front, meeting in a segment of a circle above; there is also another iron rod affixed to the back, which curves over the head of the person seated in the chair, and is connected with the other at the top, to the centre of which is fastened an iron ring for the purpose of slinging the machine into the river. It is plain and substantial, and has more the appearance of solidity than antiquity in its construction. We are told by the local historian that in the Chamberlain's books are various entries for money paid to porters for taking down the ducking-stool and assisting in the operation of cooling, by its means, the inflammable passions of some of the female inhabitants of Ipswich.

SCARBOROUGH DUCKING-STOOL.

We give a spirited sketch of the Ipswich ducking-stool, from the pencil of Campion, a local artist. It is worthy of the pencil of Hogarth, Gilray, or Cruikshank; indeed, it is often said to be the production of the last-named artist, but though after his style it is not his work.

There are traces in the Court-Book of St. George's Gild of the use of the ducking-stool at Norwich. Amongst other entries is one to the effect that in 1597 a scold was ducked three times.

IPSWICH DUCKING-STOOL.

The ducking-stool at Nottingham, in addition to being employed for correcting scolds, was used for the exposure of females of bad repute. "It consisted," says Mr. J. Potter Briscoe, F.R.H.S., "of a hollow box, which was sufficiently large to admit of two persons being exposed at the same time. Through holes in the side the heads of the culprits were placed. In fact, the Nottingham cuck-stool was similar to a pillory. The last time this ancient instrument of punishment was brought into requisition was in 1731, when the Mayor (Thomas Trigge) caused a female to be placed in it for immorality, and left her to the mercy of the mob, who ducked her so severely that her

IPSWICH DUCKING-STOOL.

death ensued shortly afterwards. The Mayor, in consequence, was prosecuted, and the Nottingham cuck-stool was ordered to be destroyed." In the

Nottinghamshire records are traces of the ducking-stool at Southwell and Retford. The example of the latter town is traced back to an unusually early period.

The old ducking-stool of King's Lynn, Norfolk, may now be seen in the Museum of that town.

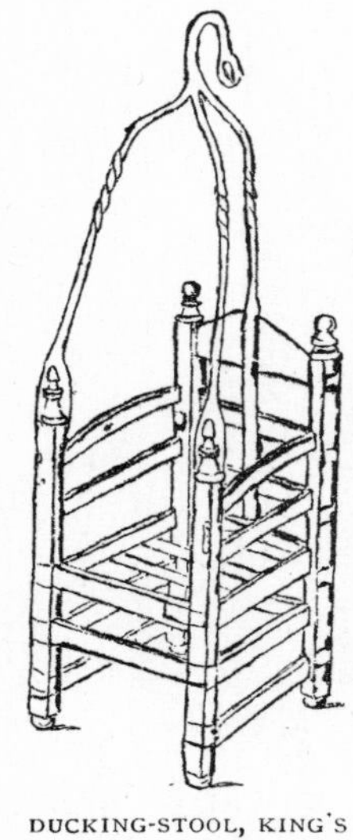

DUCKING-STOOL, KING'S LYNN.

The annals of the borough contain numerous allusions to the punishment of women. In the year 1587, it is stated that for immoral conduct, John Wanker's wife and widow Parker were both carted. It is recorded that, in 1754, "one Elizabeth Neivel stood in the pillory, and that one Hannah Clark was ducked for scolding." There is mention of a woman named Howard standing in the pillory in 1782, but no particulars are given of her crime.

In a note written for us in 1881, by Mr. R. N. Worth, the historian of Plymouth, we are told that in Devon and Cornwall the ducking-stool was the usual means employed for inflicting punishment on scolding women. At Plymouth, the ducking-stool was erected at the Barbican, a site full of historic interest. From here Sir Walter Raleigh was conducted to his long imprisonment, followed by death on the scaffold. It was here that the Pilgrim Fathers bade adieu to the shores of their native land to establish a New England across the Atlantic. As might be expected, the old municipal accounts of Plymouth contain many curious and interesting items bearing on the punishment of women. Mr. W. H. K. Wright, editor of the *Western Antiquary*, tells us that as recently as the year 1808 the last person was ducked. At Plymouth, at the present time, are preserved two ducking-chairs, one in the Athenæum and the other in the office of the Borough Surveyor. Mr. Wright has kindly supplied illustrations of both. It will be observed that the chairs are made of iron.

PLYMOUTH DUCKING-STOOL.

The last time the Bristol ducking-stool was used was, it is said, in the year 1718. The

Mayor gave instructions for the ducking of scolds, and the immersions took place at the weir.

We have numerous accounts of this engine of punishment in Lancashire. In the "Manchester Historical Recorder" we find it stated, in the year 1775: "Manchester ducking-stool in use. It was an open-bottomed chair of wood, placed upon a long pole balanced on a pivot, and suspended over the collection of water called the Pool House and Pool Fold. It was afterwards suspended over the Daubholes (Infirmary pond) and was used for the purpose of punishing scolds and prostitutes." We find, on examination of an old print, that it was similar to the example at Broadwater, of which we give a sketch. According to Mr. Richard Brooke's "Liverpool from 1775 to 1800," the ducking-stool was in use in 1779, by the authority of the magistrates. We have details of the ducking-stool at Preston, Kirkham, Burnley and other Lancashire towns.

PLYMOUTH DUCKING-STOOL.

At Wootton Bassett there was a tumbrel,

which, until within the last few years, was perfect. The chair is still preserved by the corporation of that town. We give a drawing of it from the *Wiltshire Archæological and Natural History Magazine*. It will be seen from the picture that the machine, when complete, consisted of a chair, a pair of wheels, two long poles forming shafts, and a rope attached to each shaft, at about a foot from the end. The person to be ducked was tied in

TUMBREL AT WOOTTON BASSETT.

the chair, and the machine pushed into a pond called the Weirpond, and the shafts being let go, the scold was lifted backwards into the water, the shafts flying up, and being recovered again by means of the ropes attached to them. The chair is of oak, and bears the date of 1686 on the back. In some places, millers, if detected stealing corn, were placed in the tumbrel.

The wheels of a tumbrel are preserved in

the old church of St. Mary's, Warwick, and the chair, it is said, is still in the possession of an inhabitant of the town.

At Kingston-upon-Thames ducking was not infrequent. The Chamberlain's accounts include many items relating to the subject. We are disposed to believe, from the mention of three wheels, in a payment made in 1572, that here the engine of punishment was a tumbrel. The following amounts were paid in 1572:

The making of the cucking-stool		8s.	0d.
Iron work for the same		3s.	0d.
Timber for the same...		7s.	6d.
Three brasses for the same, and three wheels		4s.	10d.
	£1	3s.	4d.

In the *London Evening Post*, April 27th to 30th, 1745, it is stated: "Last week a woman who keeps the Queen's Head alehouse, at Kingston, in Surrey, was ordered by the court to be ducked for scolding, and was accordingly placed in the chair and ducked in the river Thames, under Kingston Bridge, in the presence of 2000 to 3000 people."

We have previously mentioned the fact that at Leicester the cucking-stool was in use as early as 1467, and from some valuable information brought together by Mr. William Kelly, F.S.A., and included in his important local works, we learn that the last entry he has traced in the old accounts of the town is the following:

1768-9. Paid Mr. Elliott for a Cuckstool by order of Hall ... ... £2 0s. 0d.

Mr. Kelly refers to the scolding cart at Leicester, and describes the culprit as seated upon it, and being drawn through the town. He found in the old accounts in 1629 an item:

Paid to Frauncis Pallmer for making two wheels and one barr for the Scolding Cart ... ... ijs.

Scolding-car is another name for the tumbrel.

The latest example of Leicester cucking-stool is preserved in the local museum, and was placed there at the suggestion of Mr. Kelly.

The Leominster ducking-stool is one of the few examples still preserved. It was formerly kept in the parish church. We have an excellent drawing of it in that building from the pencil of the genial author of "Verdant Green," Cuthbert Bede. The Rev. Geo. Fyler Townsend, M.A., the erudite historian of Leominster, furnishes us with some important information on this interesting relic of the olden time. He says that it is a machine of the simplest construction. "It consists merely of a strong narrow under framework, placed on four wheels, of solid wood, about four inches in thickness, and eighteen in diameter. At one end of this framework two upright posts, about three feet in height, strongly embedded in the platform, carry a long movable beam. Each of the arms of this beam are of equal length (13

LEOMINSTER DUCKING-STOOL.

feet), and balance perfectly from the top of the post. The culprit placed in the seat naturally weighs down that one end into the water, while the other is lifted up in the air; men, however, with ropes, caused the uplifted end to rise or fall, and thus obtain a perfect see-saw. The purchase of the machine is such that the culprit can be launched forth some 16 to 18 feet into the pond or stream, while the administrators of the ducking stand on dry land. This instrument was mentioned in the ancient documents of the borough by various names, as the cucking-stoole or timbrill, or gumstole."

The latest recorded instance of the ducking-stool being used in England occurred at Leominster. In 1809, says Mr. Townsend, a woman, Jenny Pipes, alias Jane Corran, was paraded through the town on the ducking-stool, and actually ducked in the water near Kenwater Bridge, by order of the magistrates. An eye witness gave his testimony to the desert of the punishment inflicted on this occasion, in the fact that the first words of the culprit on being unfastened from the chair were oaths and curses on the magistrates. In 1817, a woman named Sarah Leeke was wheeled round the town in the chair, but not ducked, as the water was too low. Since this time, the use of the chair has been laid aside, and it is an object of curiosity, rather than of fear, to any of the spectators. During the recent restoration of Leominster Church, the ducking-stool was removed, repaired, and renovated by Mr. John Hungerford Arkwright, and is now kept at the borough gaol of the historically interesting town of Leominster.

The early English settlers in the United States introduced many of the manners and customs of their native land. The ducking-stool was soon brought into use. Mr. Henry M. Brooks, in his carefully written work, called "Strange and Curious Punishments," published in 1886, by Ticknor & Co., of Boston, gives many important details respecting punishing scolds. At the present time, in some parts of America, scolding females are liable to be punished by means of the ducking-stool. We gather from a newspaper report that in 1889, the grand jury of Jersey City—across the Hudson River from New York—caused a sensation by indicting Mrs. Mary Brady as a "common scold." Astonished lawyers hunted up their old books, and discovered that scolding is still an indictable offence in New Jersey, and that the ducking-stool is still available as a punishment for it, not having been specifically abolished when the revised statutes were adopted. In Delaware, the State next to the south of New Jersey, the whipping-post is an institution, and prisoners are sentenced to suffer at it every week. The Common Scold Law was brought from

England to Connecticut by the Puritans and settlers, and from Connecticut they carried it with them into New Jersey, which is incorrectly considered a Dutch state. In closing this chapter, we may state that a Dalziel telegram from Ottawa, published in the London newspapers of August 8th, 1890, says that Miss Annie Pope was yesterday charged before a police magistrate, under the provisions of an antiquated statute, for being a "common scold." She was committed for trial at the assizes, as the magistrate had no ducking-stool.

The Brank, or Scold's Bridle.

THE brank was an instrument employed by our forefathers for punishing scolds. It is also sometimes called the gossip's bridle, and in the Macclesfield town records it is designated "a brydle for a curste queane." In the term "queane" we have the old English synonym for a woman; now the chief woman, the Queen. The brank is not of such great antiquity as the ducking-stool, for the earliest mention of it we have been able to find in this country is in the Corporation records of Macclesfield, of the year 1623. At an earlier period, we have traces of it in Scotland. In Glasgow burgh records, it is stated that in 1574 two scolds were condemned to be "branket." The Kirk-session

records of Stirling for 1600 mention the "brankes" as a punishment for the shrew. It is generally believed that the punishment is of Continental origin.

The brank may be described simply as an iron framework which was placed on the head, enclosing it in a kind of cage; it had in front a plate of iron, which, either sharpened or covered with spikes, was so situated as to be placed in the mouth of the victim, and if she attempted to move her tongue in any way whatever, it was certain to be shockingly injured. With a brank on her head she was conducted through the streets, led by a chain, held by one of the town's officials, an object of contempt, and subjected to the jeers of the crowd and often left to their mercy. In some towns it was the custom to chain the culprit to the pillory, whipping-post, or market-cross. She thus suffered for telling her mind to some petty tyrant in office, or speaking plainly to a wrong-doer, or for taking to task a lazy, and perhaps a drunken husband.

In Yorkshire, we have only seen two branks. We give a sketch of one formerly in possession of the late Norrisson Scatcherd, F.S.A., the historian of Morley. It is now in the Leeds Philosophical

Museum, where it attracts considerable attention. It is one of the most simple and harmless examples that has come under our notice. Amongst the relics of the olden time in the Museum of the Yorkshire Philosophical Society, York, is another specimen, equally simple in its construction. It was presented by Lady Thornton to the Society in 1880, and near it may be seen thumb-screws from York Castle; leg bar, waist girdle, and wrist shackles, worn by the notorious highwayman, Dick Turpin, executed April 17th, 1739; and a leg bar, worn by another notorious highwayman, named Nevison, who suffered death on the gallows, May 4th, 1684.

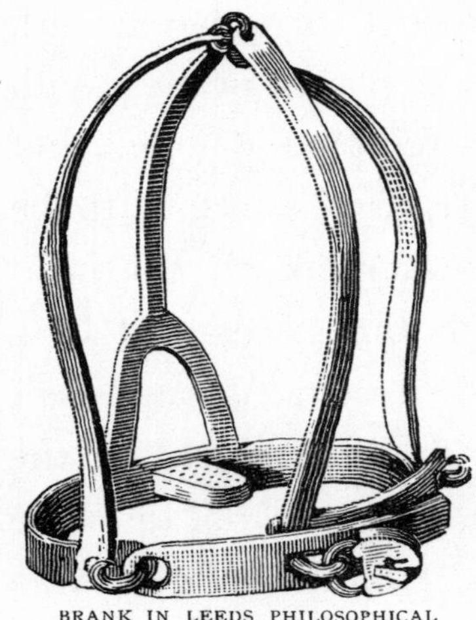

BRANK IN LEEDS PHILOSOPHICAL MUSEUM.

The brank which has received the greatest attention is the one preserved in the vestry of Walton-on-Thames Parish Church. It bears the date of 1632, and the following couplet:—

> "Chester presents Walton with a bridle
> To curb women's tongues that talk too idle."

It is traditionally said that this brank was given to Walton Parish by a person named Chester, who had, through a gossiping and lying woman of his acquaintance, lost an estate he expected to inherit from a rich relative. We are enabled to give an illustration of the Walton brank.

Dr. T. N. Brushfield described in an exhaustive manner all the Cheshire branks, in an able paper read before the Architectural, Archæo-

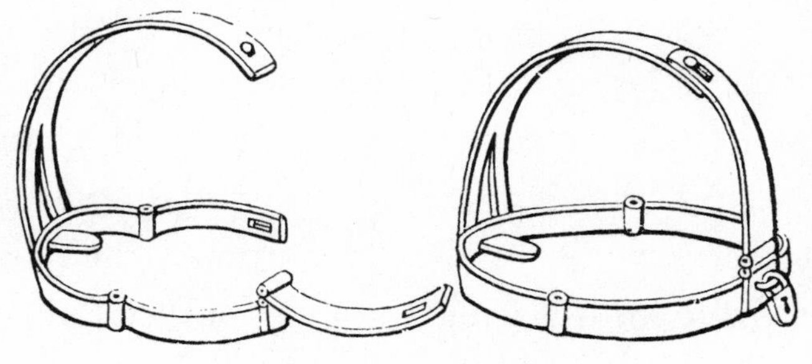

BRANK AT WALTON-ON-THAMES.

logical, and Historic Society of Chester, and published in 1858. We are unable to direct attention to all the branks noticed by Dr. Brushfield, but cannot refrain from presenting the following account of the one at Congleton, which is preserved in the Town Hall of that ancient borough. "It was," we are informed, "formerly in the hands of the town jailor, whose services were not infrequently called into requisition. In the old-fashioned, half-timbered houses in the borough, there was generally fixed on one side of the large open fire-places a hook, so that, when a man's wife indulged her scolding propensities, the husband sent for the town jailor to bring the bridle, and had her bridled and chained to the hook until she promised to behave herself better for the future. I have seen one of these hooks, and have often heard husbands say to their wives: 'If you don't rest with your tongue I'll send for the bridle and hook you up.' The Mayor and Justices frequently brought the instrument into use; for when women were brought before them charged with street-brawling, and insulting the constables and others while in the discharge of their duty, they have ordered them to be bridled and led through the borough by the jailor. The last time this bridle was publicly used was in 1824, when a woman was brought before the Mayor (Bulkeley Johnson, Esq.) one Monday, charged with scolding and using harsh language to the churchwardens and constables as they went, on the Sunday morning, round the town to see that all the public-houses were empty and closed during divine service. On examination, a Mr. Richard Edwards stated on oath 'that on going round the town with the churchwardens on the previous day, they met the woman (Ann Runcorn) in a place near 'The Cockshoot,' and that immediately seeing them she commenced a sally of abuse, calling them all the scoundrels and rogues she could lay her tongue to; and telling them 'it would look better of them if they would look after their own houses rather than go looking after other folk's, which were far better than their own.' After other abuse of a like character, they thought it only right to apprehend her, and so brought her before the Bench on the following day. The Mayor then delivered the following sentence: 'That it is the unanimous decision of the Mayor and Justices that the prisoner (Ann Runcorn) there and then have the town's bridle for scolding women put upon her, and that she be led by the magistrate's clerk's clerk through every street in the town, as an example to all scolding women; and that the Mayor and magistrates were much obliged to the churchwardens for bringing the case before them.'" "In this case," Mr. Warrington, who furnished Dr. Brushfield with the foregoing information, adds: "I both heard the evidence and saw the decision carried out. The bridle was put on the woman, and she was then led through the town by one Prosper Haslam, the town clerk's clerk, accompanied by hundreds of the inhabitants; and on her return to the Town Hall the bridle was taken off in the presence of the Mayor, magistrates, constables, churchwardens, and assembled inhabitants."

In Cheshire, at the present time, there are traces of thirteen branks, and at Stockport is the most brutal example of the English branks. "It will be observed," says the local historian, Dr. Henry Heginbotham, J.P., "that the special characteristic of this brank is the peculiar construction of the tongue-plate or gag. It is about two inches long, having at the end, as may be seen in the engraving, a ball, into which is inserted a number of sharp iron pins, three on the upper surface, three on the lower, and two pointing backwards. These could not fail to pin the tongue, and effectually silence the noisiest brawler. At the fore part of the collar, there is an iron chain, with a leathern thong attached,

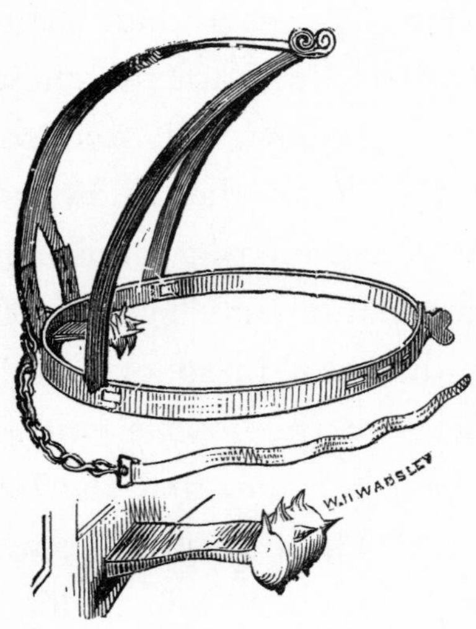

BRANK AT STOCKPORT.

by which the offender was led for public gaze through the market-place." It was formerly on market days exhibited in front of the house of the person who had charge of it, as a warning to scolding or swearing women. Dr. Heginbotham states that: "There is no evidence of its having been actually used for many years, but there is testimony to the fact, that within the last forty years the brank was brought to a termagant market woman, who was effectually silenced by its threatened application."

We are indebted to Mr. Alfred Burton for a drawing of the Macclesfield brank. Dr. Brushfield describes this as "a respectable-looking brank." He tells us that "the gag is plain, and the end of it is turned down; there is only one band which passes over the head, and is hinged to the hoops; a temporary joint exists at the upper part, and ample provision is made for readily adjusting it to any description of head. The chain still remains attached to the hoop. About the year 1858, Mr. Swinnerton informed Dr. Brushfield that he had never seen it used, but that at the petty sessions it had often been produced *in terrorem*, to stay the volubility of a woman's tongue; and that a threat by a magistrate to order its appliance had always proved sufficient to abate the garrulity of the most determined scold."

Towards the close of the first quarter of the present century, the brank was last used at Altrincham. A virago, who caused her neigh-

BRANK AT MACCLESFIELD.

bours great trouble, was frequently cautioned in vain respecting her conduct, and as a last resource she was condemned to walk through the town wearing the brank. She refused to move, and it was finally decided to wheel her in a barrow through the principal streets of the town, round the market-place, and to her own home. The punishment had the desired effect, and for the remainder of her life she kept a quiet tongue.

There are many traces of the brank in Lancashire. Mr. W. E. A. Axon informs us that his father remembers the brank being used at Manchester at the commencement of the present century. Kirkham had its brank for scolds, in addition to a ducking-stool. We find, in the same county, traces of the brank at Holme, in the Forest of Rossendale. In the accounts of the Greave for the Forest of Rossendale for 1691-2 is an entry of the true antiquarian cast :

Item, for a Bridle for scouldinge women, ... 2s. 6d.

In "Some Obsolete Peculiarities of English Law," by William Beamont, the author gives particulars respecting the Warrington brank. "Hanging up in our museum," says Mr. Beamont, "may be seen a representation of a withered female face wearing the brank or scold's bridle; one of which instruments, as inflexible as iron and ingenuity can make it, for keeping an unruly tongue quiet by mechanical means, hangs up beside it; and almost within the time of living memory, Cicily Pewsill, an inmate of the workhouse, and a notorious scold, was seen wearing this disagreeable head-gear in the streets of Warrington for half-an-hour or more. . . . Cicily Pewsill's case still lingers in tradition, as the last occasion of its application in Warrington, and it will soon pass into history."

The Rev. J. Clay told Mr. William Dobson that since his connection with Preston House of Correction the brank was put on a woman there, but the matter coming to the knowledge of the Home Secretary, its further use was prohibited, and to make sure of the barbarous practice being discontinued the brank itself was ordered to be sent to London. A second brank was kept in the prison, principally formed of leather, but with an iron tongue-piece.*

At the north country town of Morpeth a brank is still preserved. The following is a record of its use: "Dec. 3, 1741, Elizabeth, wife of George Holborn, was punished with the branks for two hours, at the Market Cross, Morpeth, by order of Mr. Thomas Gait and Mr. George Nicholls, then bailiffs, for scandalous and opprobrious language to several persons in the town, as well as to the said bailiffs."

* Dobson's "Preston in the Olden Time," 1857.

Staffordshire supplies several notable examples of the brank. They were formerly kept at Hamstall Ridware, Beaudesart, Lichfield, Walsall, and at Newcastle-under-Lyme. The branks in the two towns last named are alluded to by the celebrated Dr. Plot, the old historian of the county, in an amusing manner. "We come to

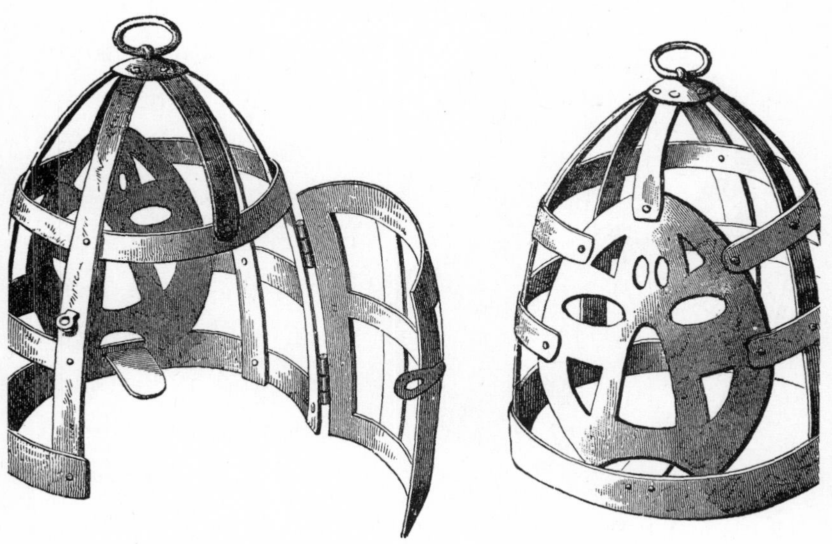

BRANK AT THE MANOR HOUSE, HAMSTALL RIDWARE.

the arts that respect mankind," says Plot, "amongst which, as elsewhere, the civility of precedence must be allowed to the woman, and that as well in punishments as favours. For the former, whereof they have such a peculiar artifice at Newcastle [under Lyme] and Walsall for correcting of scolds, which it does, too, so effectually and so very safely, that I look upon it as much to be preferred to the cucking-stool, which not only endangers the health of the party, but also gives her tongue liberty 'twixt every dip, to neither of which is this at all liable, it being such a bridle for the tongue as not only quite deprives them of speech, but brings shame for the transgression, and humility thereupon, before 'tis taken off. Which, being an instrument scarce heard of, much less seen, I have here presented it to the reader's view [here follows a reference to a plate] as it was taken from the original one, made of iron, at Newcastle-under-Lyme, wherein the letter *a* shows the jointed collar that comes round the neck; *b*, *c*, the loops and staples to let it out and in, according to the bigness and slenderness of the neck; *d*, the jointed semicircle that comes over the head, made forked at one end to let through the nose, and *e*, the plate-iron that

BRANK AT LICHFIELD.

is put into the mouth and keeps down the tongue. Which, being put upon the offender by order of the magistrate, and fastened with a padlock behind, she is led through the town by an officer, to her shame, nor is it taken off until after the party begins to show all external signs imaginable of humiliation and amendment." This brank afterwards passed into the hands of Mr. Joseph Mayer, F.S.A. founder of the Museum at Liverpool.

It is pleasing to record the fact that there is only trace of one brank belonging to Derbyshire —a circumstance which speaks well for its men and women. The latter have for a long period borne exemplary characters. Philip Kinder, in the preface of his projected "History of Derbyshire," written about the middle of the seventeenth century, alludes to them. "The country-women here," says Kinder, "are chaste and sober, and very diligent in their housewifery; they hate idleness, love and obey their husbands; only in some of the great towns many of the seeming sanctificators used to follow the Presbyterian gang, and on a lecture day put on their best rayment, and doo hereby take occasion to goo a gossipping. Your merry wives of Bentley will sometimes look in ye glass, chirpe a cupp merrily, yet not indecently. In the Peak they are much given to dance after the bagpipes—almost every towne hath a bagpipe in it." "The Chesterfield brank," says Mr. Llewellyn Jewitt, "is a remarkably good example, and has the additional interest of bearing a date. It is nine inches in height, and six inches and three-quarters across the hoop. It consists of a hoop of iron, hinged on either side and fastening behind, and a band, also of iron, passing over the head from back to front, and opening in front to admit the nose of the woman whose misfortune it was to wear it. The mode of putting it on would be thus: the brank would be opened by throwing back the sides of the hoop, and the hinder part of the band by means of the hinges, C, F, F. The constable, or other official, would then stand in

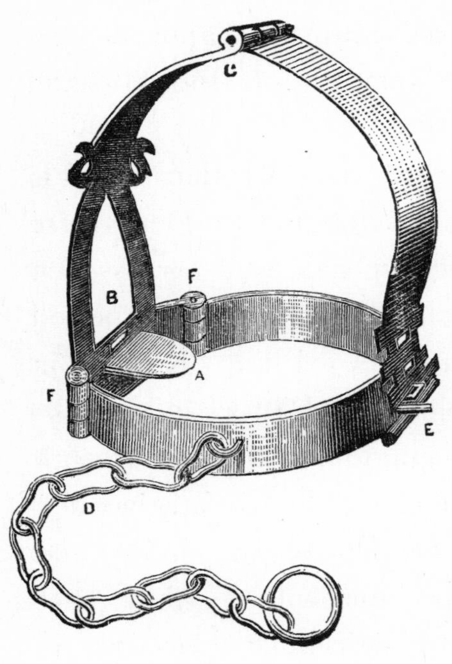

CHESTERFIELD BRANK.

front of his victim, and force the knife, or plate, A, into her mouth, the divided band passing on either side of the nose, which would protrude through the opening, B. The hoop would then be closed behind, the band brought down from the top to the back of the head, and fastened down upon it, at E, and thus the cage would at once be firmly and immovably fixed so long as her tormentors might think fit. On the left side is a chain, D, one end of which is attached to the hoop, and at the other end is a ring, by which the victim was led, or by which she was, at pleasure, attached to a post or wall. On front of the brank are the initials 'T.C.,' and the date '1688'—the year of the 'Glorious Revolution'—the year of all years memorable in the annals of Chesterfield and the little village of Whittington, closely adjoining, in which the Revolution was planned. Strange that an instrument of brutal and tyrannical torture should be made and used at Chesterfield at the same moment that the people should be plotting for freedom at the same place. The brank was formerly in the old poor-house at Chesterfield, and came into the hands of Mr. Weale, the assistant Poor-law Commissioner, who presented it to Lady Walsham. It is (August,

1860) still in the hands of Sir John Walsham, Bart., and the drawing from which the accompanying woodcut is executed was kindly made and furnished to me by Miss Dulcy Bell, Sir John's sister-in-law." *

The Leicester brank is similar to the one at Chesterfield. At the back of the hoop is a chain about twelve inches long. It was formerly kept in the Leicester borough gaol.

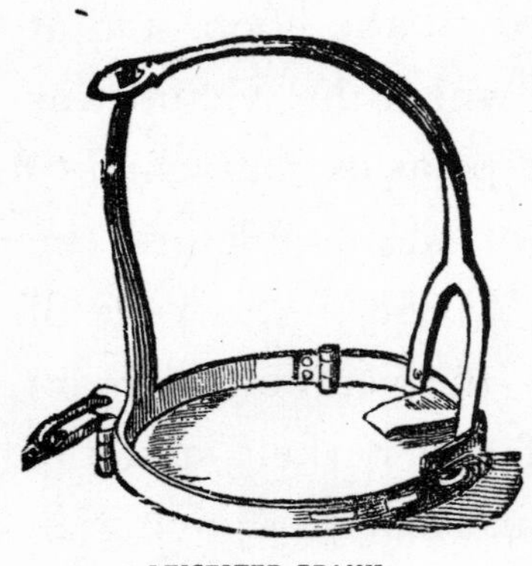

LEICESTER BRANK.

In the year 1821, Judge Richardson gave orders for a brank to be destroyed which was kept ready and most probably frequently used at the County Hall, Nottingham. We gather from a note furnished by Mr. J. Potter Briscoe a curious circumstance in connection with this brank —that it was used to subdue the unruly tongues of the sterner sex, as well as those of noisy females. James Brodie, a blind beggar who was executed on the 15th July, 1799, for the murder of his boy-guide, in the Nottingham Forest, was the last person punished with the brank. During his

* "The Reliquary," October, 1860.

imprisonment, prior to execution, he was so noisy that the brank was called into requisition, to do what he refused to do himself, namely, to hold his tongue.

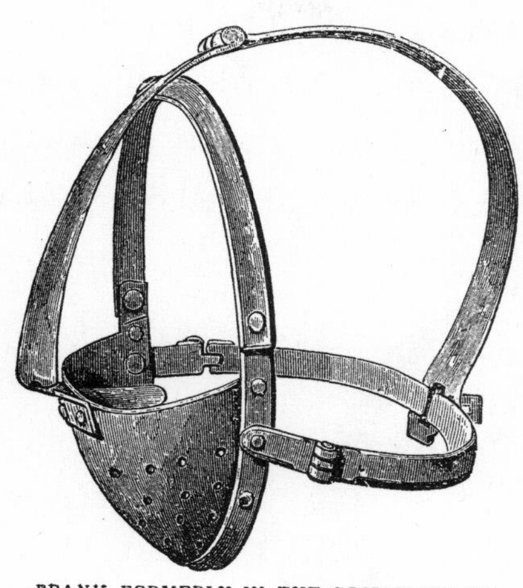

BRANK FORMERLY IN THE POSSESSION OF MR. CARRINGTON.

Here is a picture of a brank formerly in the possession of the late Mr. F. A. Carrington, the well-known antiquary. It is supposed to belong to the period of William III. Mr. Carrington could not give any history of this curious relic of the olden time.

At Doddington Park, Lincolnshire, a brank is preserved, and is of a decidedly foreign appearance. It will be noticed that it bears some resemblance to the peculiar long-snouted visor of the bascinets, occasionally worn

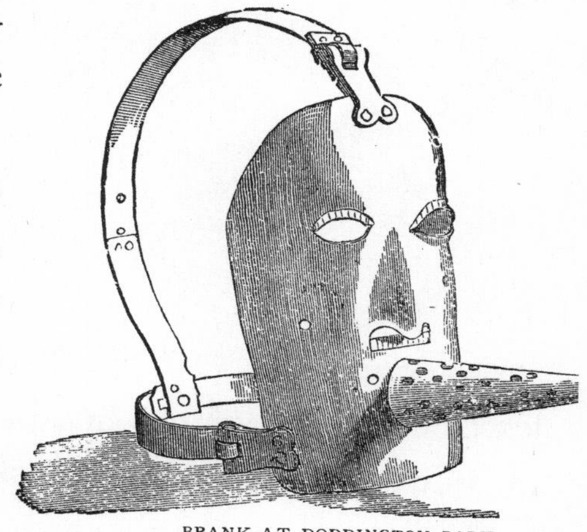

BRANK AT DODDINGTON PARK.

in the reign of Richard II. No historical particulars are known respecting this grotesque brank.

In the Ashmolean Museum at Oxford, a curious brank may be seen. It is not recorded in the catalogue of the collection by whom it was presented, or where it was previously used; it is

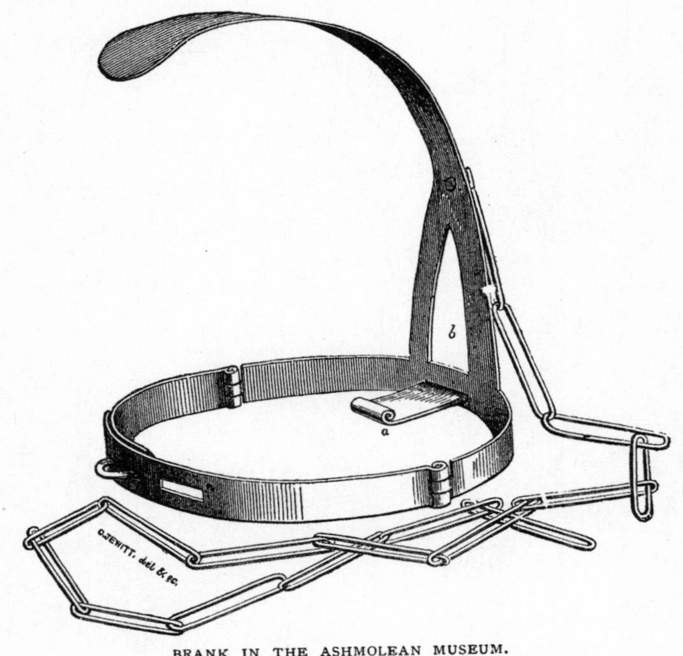

BRANK IN THE ASHMOLEAN MUSEUM.

described as a "a gag or brank, formerly used with the ducking-stool, as a punishment for scolds." It will be noticed that a chain is attached to the front of this brank, so that the poor unfortunate woman, in addition to being gagged, had the mortification of being led by the nose through the town. The gag is marked *a*, and *b* is the aperture for the nose.

A curious engine of torture may be seen in the Ludlow Museum, and we give an illustration of it. It belongs to a class of engines far more formidable than branks. A description of this head-piece appears in the *Archæological Journal* for September, 1856, from the pen of Mr. W. J. Bernard Smith. "The powerful screwing apparatus," says Mr. Smith, "seems calculated to force the iron mask with torturing effect upon the brow of the victim; there are no eye-holes, but concavities in their places, as though to allow for the starting of the eye-balls under violent pressure. There is a strong bar with a square hole, evidently intended to fasten the criminal against a wall, or perhaps to the pillory; and I have heard it said that these instruments

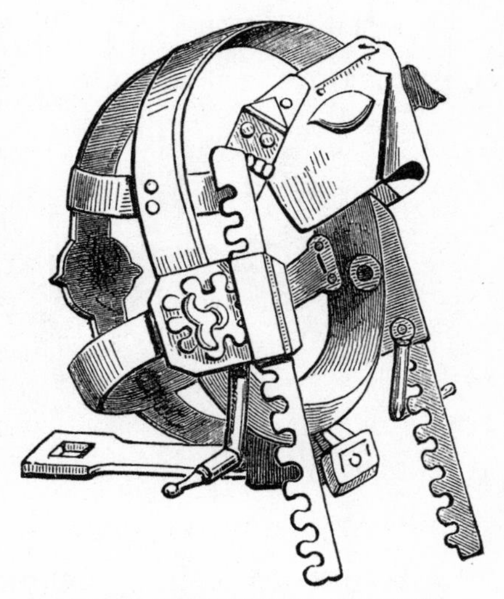

ENGINE OF TORTURE IN THE LUDLOW MUSEUM.

were used to keep the head steady during the infliction of branding." A curious instrument of punishment, belonging to the same class as that at Ludlow, is described at some length, with an illustration, in "Worcester in Olden Times," by John Noake (London, 1849). The picture and description have been frequently reproduced.

Several Shropshire branks remain at the present time. The one at Shrewsbury does not

SHREWSBURY BRANK.

appear to be of any great antiquity. Its form is simple and its character harmless. This bridle was at one time in constant use in Shrewsbury, and there are those yet living whose memories are sufficiently good to carry them back to the days when the effects of the application of the brank in question were to be seen, rather than, as now, imagined. The year cannot be ascertained when this brank was first worn, but it is known to have been last used in 1846.*

* Morris's "Obsolete Punishments of Shropshire."

At Oswestry are two branks, one belonging to the Corporation, and the other is in the store-room of the Workhouse. The Rector of Whitchurch has in his possession a brank, which was formerly used by the town and union authorities. At Market Drayton are two branks: one is the property of the Lord of the Manor, and the other formerly belonged to the Dodcot Union. The Market Drayton brank, and also the one at Whitchurch, have on each a revolving wheel at the end of the gag or tongue-plate. In bygone times, the brank was frequently used for correcting unmanageable paupers.

At Edinburgh, in the Museum of the Society of Antiquaries of Scotland, is a brank said to be from a town in East Fifeshire, having a rowel-shaped gag. In the year 1560, it was decided by the Town Council of Edinburgh, that all persons found guilty of blasphemy should be punished by the iron brank. In North Britain, it appears to have been used for punishing persons guilty of immorality. On the 7th October, the Kirk-Session of Canongate sentenced David Persoun, convicted of this offence, to be "brankit for four hours," while his associate in guilt, Isobel Mountray, was "banisit the gait," that is, expelled from the parish. Only a week previously, the same Kirk-Session had issued a proclamation that all women found guilty of this lawlessness "be brankit six houris at the croce."

We close this chapter by directing attention to the Bishop's brank, kept at St. Andrews, respecting which a singular story is told. A woman in a humble walk of life, named Isabel Lindsay, stood up in the parish church of St. Andrews, during the time of divine service, when Archbishop Sharp was preaching, and declared that when he was a college student he was guilty of an illicit amour with her. She was arrested for this statement, and brought before the Kirk-Sessions, and by its members sentenced "to appear for a succession of Sundays on the repentance stool, wearing the brank."

Riding the Stang.

THE ancient custom of riding the stang still lingers in some remote parts of the country. Holding delinquents up to ridicule was a favourite mode of punishment practised by our forefathers, and riding the stang was the means generally employed for punishing husbands who beat their wives, or allowed themselves to be henpecked, or were profligate in their conduct. There are various designations for the custom. In Yorkshire, riding the stang is the name used; in Scotland the same term is applied; in the South of England skimmington-riding is the title generally employed, and on the Continent it is known by other appellations.

The mode of carrying out the ceremony is as follows: A man having beaten his wife, the young men of the village assume the attitude of public censors, and arrangements are made for riding the stang three nights in succession. A trumpeter blows his horn loud and long as day gives way to night, and the villagers are brought together. A pole or a ladder is procured, and the most witty man in the village is placed thereon, mounted shoulder-high, and carried in great state through the streets. In one hand he has a large key or stick, and in the other a dripping-pan, and

RIDING THE STANG.

leads the music of the crowd. Men, women, and children join in the fun, and beat kettles, pans, pots, or anything else that will make a noise; tin whistles, horns, and trumpets are blown, the noise produced being better imagined than described. As soon as all is ready, a start is made, and about every fifty yards the procession stops, and the mounted man proclaims at the top of his voice a rhyme suited to the nature of the offence, somewhat as follows :

> "Ran, tan, tan ; ran, tan, tan,
> To the sound of this pan ;
> This is to give notice that Tom Trotter
> Has beaten his good woman !
> For what, and for why?
> Because she ate when she was hungry,
> And drank when she was dry.
> Ran, tan, ran, tan, tan ;
> Hurrah—hurrah ! for this good wo-man !
> He beat her, he beat her, he beat her indeed,
> For spending a penny when she had need.
> He beat her black, he beat her blue ;
> When Old Nick gets him, he'll give him his due ;
> Ran, tan, tan ; ran, tan, tan ;
> We'll send him there in this old frying-pan ;
> Hurrah—hurrah ! for his good wo-man !"

We have an example noted at Sutton, near Hull, in August, 1877. It was given with great spirit by a youth, mounted after the customary manner on a ladder, to the evident enjoyment of a large gathering of the inhabitants, who were enraged at the brutal treatment of a woman by her husband :

"Here we come with a ran, dan, dang:
It's not for you, nor for me, we ride this stang;
But for ———, whose wife he did bang.
He banged her, he banged her, he banged her indeed:
He banged her, poor creature, before she stood need.
He took up neither tipstaff nor stower,
But with his fist he knocked her backwards ower;
He kicked her, he punched her, till he made her cry,
And to finish all, he gave her a black eye.
Now, all you good people that live in this row,
We would have you take warning, for this is our law:
If any of you, your wives you do bang,
We're sure, we're sure, to ride you the stang."

"Last night," says the *Sunderland Daily Post* of March 1st, 1887, "some excitement was caused in Northallerton by the celebration of the old custom of 'riding the stang,' which is to expose some one guilty of gross immoral practices, and of a breach of sacred matrimonial rights. Some hundreds of people followed the conveyance, in which two effigies were erected and exhibited through the principal streets. At intervals, a person in the conveyance shouted out in rhyme their object, and said they fully intended to make a complete celebration of the custom, which is to 'ride the stang' three nights in succession, and on the last night to burn the effigies on the green near the church."

The stang was ridden at the ancient town of Hedon, 18th, 19th, and 20th February, 1889.

The house of the culprit is visited several times each night, and the proceedings kept up three nights in succession, and a circuit of the church is also made, as it is believed that those taking part in the ceremony will not be amenable to the law, if they do not omit this part of the custom. If the offence is a very serious one, the offender is burnt in effigy before his own door. In the olden days, the offender himself was often compelled to ride the stang.

Several of the old poets refer to this ancient usage. Allan Ramsay, in one of his poems, published in 1721, says:

"They frae a barn a kaber raught
And mounted wi' a bang,
Betwisht twa's shoulders, and sat straught,
Upon't and *rade the stang*
On her that day."

Mr. Geo. Roberts, of Lyme Regis, forwarded to Sir Walter Scott some interesting notes on skimmington-riding. He informed Sir Walter that in the South of England: "About dusk two individuals, one armed with a skimmer and the other with a ladle, came out of some obscure street attended by a crowd, whose laughter, huzzas, etc., emulate the well-known *charivari* of the French. The two performers are sometimes in a cart, at other times on a donkey; one personating the wife, the other the husband. They beat each other furiously with the culinary weapons above described, and, warmed by the applause and presence of so many spectators (for all turn out to see a skimmington), their dialogue attains a freedom, except using surnames, only comparable with their gestures. On arriving at the house of the parties represented in the moving drama, animation is at its height: the crowd usually stay at the spot some minutes, and then traverse the town. The performers are remunerated by the spectators: the parties who parade the streets with the performers sweep with brooms the doors of those who are likely to require a similar visitation."

Dr. King, in his "Miscellany," thus refers to the subject:

> "When the young people ride the skimmington,
> There is a general trembling in the town;
> Not only he for whom the party rides
> Suffers, but they sweep other doors besides;
> And by the hieroglyphic does appear
> That the good woman is the master there."

According to Douce, *skimmington* is derived from *skimming-ladle*, used in the ceremony.

In Butler's "Hudibras," considerable attention is paid to the custom. A few of the lines are as follow:

"And now the cause of all their fear,
By slow degrees approached so near,
Of horns, and pans, and dogs, and boys,
And kettle-drums whose sullen dub,
Sounds like the hooping of a tub;

. . . . . .

And followed with a world of tall lads,
That merry ditties troll'd and ballads.

. . . . . .

Next pans and kettles of all keys,
From trebles down to double base:

. . . . . .

And at fit periods the whole rout
Set up their throat with clamorous shout."

A notice of an old Welsh ceremony appeared in the *Liverpool Mercury* on March 15th, 1887, and it will not be without interest to reproduce it. "That ancient Welsh custom," says the writer, "now nearly obsolete, known as riding the ceffyl pren—*Anglicé*, 'wooden-horse'—and intended to operate as a wholesome warning to faithless wives and husbands, was revived on Saturday night in an Anglesey village some three miles from

Llangefni. The individual who had drawn upon himself the odium of his neighbours had parted from his wife, and was alleged to be persistent in his attentions to another female. On Saturday night a large party surrounded the house, and compelled him to get astride a ladder, carrying him shoulder-high through the village, stopping at certain points to allow the womankind to wreak their vengeance upon him. This amusement was kept up for some time until the opportune arrival of a sergeant of police from Llangefni, who rescued the unlucky wight."

Index.